D0294495

The Calling of a Cuckoo

To Angie,

On your ordination
as Deacon in the
Church of God.

With our prayers and
best wishes.

Robert

Bill

July 2005.

Also by David Jenkins

A Guide to the Debate about God, Lutterworth Press 1966

The Glory of Man, SCM Press 1967

Living with Questions, SCM Press 1969

What is Man?, SCM Press 1970

The Contradiction of Christianity, SCM Press 1976

God, Miracle and the Church of England, SCM Press 1987

God, Politics and the Future, SCM Press 1988

God, Jesus and Life in the Spirit, SCM Press 1988

Still Living with Questions, SCM Press 1990

Free to Believe, BBC Books 1991

Market Whys and Human Wherefores, Cassell 2000

The Calling of a Cuckoo

Not Quite an Autobiography

David E. Jenkins
former Bishop of Durham

continuum
LONDON • NEW YORK

Continuum
The Tower Building, 11 York Road, London SE1 7NX
15 East 26th Street, New York, NY 10010

Copyright © David Edward Jenkins 2002
All rights reserved. No part of this publication may be reproduced
or transmitted in any form or by any means, electronic or mechanical, including
photocopying, recording or any information storage or retrieval system, without
prior permission in writing from the publishers.

First published in hardback 2002
Reprinted 2003
First published in paperback 2003

British Library Cataloguing in Publication Data
A catalogue record for this is available
from the British Library

ISBN 0 8264 4991 3 (hardback)
ISBN 0 8264 7099 8 (paperback)

Typeset by Kenneth Burnley, Wirral, Cheshire
Printed and bound in Great Britain by MPG Books Ltd, Bodmin

Contents

Preface

This is not only an autobiography. It is a reflection and manifesto directed personally by what happened to me as I plunged enthusiastically and, as I thought, faithfully into the unexpected call to be Bishop of Durham. I had received an invitation in my sixtieth year to enter on a decade of Christian ministry in a far wider and more public sphere than I had so far experienced, or with which I had been closely engaged.

On being designated bishop I entered into an exploration and a series of engagements which have both threatened and eventually enlarged the Christian faith which I have enjoyed ever since I was a boy. The enlargement of that faith is what I begin to set out in the closing chapters of this book.

Most of the book is about my struggles with, and increasing disillusionment over, the current state of the Church of England. This disillusionment has spread for me to the churches at large, but the focus is, naturally, on the Church of England, as for ten years I held the post of its fourth most senior bishop, whose seniority entitled me to an automatic seat in the House of Lords. I found myself more and more forced to the conclusion that the Church of England, in its present quarrelsome and institutionally obsolescent state, is just not fit or able to share, spread and serve the Christian gospel of the future which is offered to humanity by the God of the Bible, who is the God known in and through Jesus Christ and the God active in the Holy Spirit.

Through my reflections on all this as in retirement I prepared to write this book, I generated my own particular crisis of faith. The Church of England was the church where I had come to realize my faith and to learn how to worship. It was the church which recognized my strongly felt call to a priestly and missionary service. And it was the church which endorsed that recognition by ordaining me to the priesthood – and then ultimately by consecrating me as a bishop. If this church kept on providing evidence for me that obliged me to judge that somehow or other, and in too many ways, it was too often off-beam with regard to both faith and reality, then what was the status and validity of my own faith? Was I just persisting in singing a hymn which really amounted to whistling an outmoded theme in the dark?

This book is my answer to my own problem. I have agreed with so many of the reasons that the atheists give for not believing – not least the behaviour and demands of so many of the self-styled faithful. But I remain reassured that the atheists are wrong. Now my hope, my witness and my prayers are directed to persuading the companies of believers – and especially the assertively certain believers – to relax, believe a little less and collaborate a good deal more, not on defending the faith but with the aim of sharing the faith widely in service, collaboration and hope. If God is as he is in the Bible, in Jesus, and in the Holy Spirit, then faith in him is directly and perpetually concerned with the hopeful and worthwhile (and it may well be worshipful) future of all of us as human beings.

However, I must add that I have been marvellously helped and held in the faith, not least in my most difficult moments, by so many personal friends, supporters, enquirers and acquaintances, many of them within the Church of England itself, as well as on broader fronts. Moreover, I am constantly upheld and encouraged by what I must dare to call 'a great cloud of witnesses'. So many people within the churches, on the fringe of the churches and further afield seem to respond, sympathetically, encouragingly and even hopefully, to the questions and explorations which form so dynamic and searching a part of my own pilgrimage. Surely the churches should relax and let God enable us to take far more risks, find far more allies, and join in a much deeper and broader company of pilgrims in order to share with God with a view to his future. I am sure that, under God, the Church of England as I understand it – and indeed, the whole Anglican Communion – deserves a more open, hopeful and relaxed approach to God as he is in Jesus, through the Spirit. The Anglican way has much to say for it in keeping many strands of devotion, understanding and explanation going while never insisting that any one of them is either the only true one or the one which has really got there. True devotion is not about exuding certainty but about following up in fellowship, worship and hope, a future that is always to be enlarged in the way that God's love promises to bring to fulfilment.

Finally, as a fitting close to this preface, I must set on record my immense gratitude to my daughter Rebecca. As an author in her own right and under pressure to complete a book of her own she has worked tirelessly and with great skill to turn my sketchy sentences into coherent and cogent prose. In her careful and cheerful support she is indeed her mother's daughter. My debt to my wife is recorded in Chapter 14.

D E J
6 August 2002
The Feast of the Transfiguration

Introduction
Is it a mistake to take God
for granted?

Ever since I was a little boy I have simply believed in God. I discovered this belief as a conscious matter of engagement, response and will when I was told, at the age of ten, that Jesus showed that God was for me. It was made clear to me that God was for me, because God is for all, because God is love. In Jesus God was especially and particularly demonstrating his divine dynamic of love as an invitation and assistance to us human beings to enable us to develop our own dynamic of love. I knew something about love because it was clear to me that my mother loved me, with the support of my father, who kept our home going in a very friendly way. At the age of ten this was all very simple and obvious – and promised to be wonderful.

At the same age I began to understand that human nature also involved a different and, indeed, conflicting dynamic – labelled 'sin' in the overall story of God's dealings with human beings. It was the contest with sin that provided the substance and dynamic of the Bible. I cannot say that as a teenager I had a deep and overwhelming sense of my own personal sinfulness, but it was obvious to me that there was a great deal wrong with the world. I could see that much of this wrongness and misery was caused by human beings. And at the strictly personal level, in the course of life I myself became involved in actions and events about which it was more appropriate to be ashamed than proud. This problem of the pressure of this destructive wrongness in a world that my developing Christian faith saw was basically about love became all the more acute when the Second World War finally broke out. I was fourteen years old at the time.

Looking back over the early days of my conscious faith from a perspective of over sixty years of further experience and reflection, I must be liable to read into my earliest experiences more than I knew or felt at the time. Nonetheless, I believe that from my schooldays I did have some inkling that if there were to be any credible 'saviour', embodying the possibilities of the dynamic of God's love and overcoming the counter-dynamic of human sin, then that saviour would have to be a suffering one. For a dynamic of conquering love could only achieve victory by something more akin to self-sacrifice than to dominating conquest. Jesus' crucifixion was therefore of central significance to my faith in God. It lay at the core of a practical sense that was growing in me that God was truly real and involved with the earthly realities that were my environment and experience. These thoughts and that understanding produced in me a belief that my life was about worshipping this God and Saviour. I felt drawn to finding out what I could about this God and working to share this worship, pilgrimage and growth in knowledge with other people.

I therefore found myself with a discovery that amounted to a decision that I was called by God to be a missionary and a priest. I embarked upon the formal and institutional steps necessary to register myself as an ordinand with the Church of England authorities while I was still at school. The war intervened, and I was called up into the army in the autumn of 1943. As a result, I ended up attending a Church of England ordination conference in Bangalore in India sometime in 1946. I returned home after the war and the next year took up a scholarship at The Queen's College, Oxford, as an ordinand and candidate for the priesthood.

That, in the briefest outline, is a preliminary account of the launch of my faith in God. To the best of my recollection, as my life went on I was never forced into any fundamental questioning of the assurance of this faith for the greater part of my life. In common with most of my generation, in the war I was faced with vivid illustrations of the wrongness in this world. At the age of twenty-one I was serving as an officer in the Royal Artillery seconded to the Tenth Indian Field Regiment, Royal Indian Artillery. In 1946 we were moving the regiment southwards through Central India to a large mustering area near Secunderabad, where units were to dispose of their weapons and equipment in preparation for disbandment. For two days we passed through a cholera-stricken area. People lay in charpoys outside their huts and homes simply dying. We were ordered to drive through without stopping. I can still remember the precautions we were told to take as we moved past at a steady pace. The experience left me with plenty to think about. But I have to admit that it was not at the time a challenge to my Christian faith. The problem, as I then perceived it, was how I should understand and cope with the facts before me in and by my faith. The problem posed to me was not, 'How can one have faith in a God of love in such a world?'

My experience was the same with questions arising from my conversations on religious matters with fellow officers, Hindu, Muslim and Parsee. Here were matters to be enquired into in faith. It did not occur to me that my faith was challenged or threatened by the existence of these different faith perspectives. I must also confess that I did not feel any urgent need to make attempts at conversion either. It was an integral part of my belief in God that I was assured that God would provide me with sufficient resources to see me through challenges to, or apparent contradictions of, my faith in him. In my experience I was supplied with these resources from the earliest days of my self-conscious believing through fellow believers, through our exploration of the Bible and through my own researches, alongside my experiences of prayer, worship and reflection. All these ways of faith were personal – sometimes shared with other believers and searchers, and sometimes very intensely and intimately within my own heart, mind and will.

This book is the result of fifty years of simple believing in God. These 'fifty years' are a round figure for the years of my life between the age of ten or eleven, when I became self-consciously aware of my believing in God, and my receiving an invitation from the Prime Minister to accept appointment to the Bishopric of Durham. When the invitation arrived in February 1984 I had just entered my sixtieth year. My wife and I decided within twenty-four hours that I had to accept this invitation. It was so obviously in strict continuity with my discovery as a boy that I was given belief in God and a call to serve him.

The Prime Minister's invitation to a wider and more public sphere of engagement in the life of the Church of England and in society at large was unexpected. As I have said, I was in my sixtieth year, comfortably established in my job as Professor of Theology at Leeds University. Until the letter arrived my wife and I assumed that retirement would be the next stage in our lives – perhaps within the next three to five years. The letter from Downing Street landed on the mat carrying an unexpected extension of the range and scope of my ministry for up to another ten years (bishops, like other clergy, must retire by the age of seventy). The possibilities promised to be exciting, if demanding. To have such a challenge at this stage of my life seemed a great privilege indeed: an undeserved but fitting climax to the belief in God which had been integral to (although by no means properly integrated into) my life since I was a boy. I had taken God for granted, and God had granted me this.

I will discuss what I did with this opportunity later. However, the motive for writing this book stems not from what I did and said as Bishop of Durham, but from the responses I elicited and the opposition to what I did and said.

Within a few weeks of the announcement of my appointment I had become the 'controversial Bishop of Durham'. By my first Christmas in office I had even been tagged the 'Bishop of Blasphemy'. Moreover, the seed of this media-magnified response lay in the reaction of fellow Christians to what I was doing and saying. It was this response that generated my need and desire to write this book.

The faith that caused me to take God for granted had led me, in good faith, to take up an extension of my calling into the public office of a senior bishop in the Church of England. The result was an explosion of opposition from a wide range of Christians defending the faith and denouncing me. At the same time I also experienced a very wide and moving range of support combined with a positive interest in what I was attempting to do. Indeed, in all the waves of correspondence that arose from each new, or renewed, episode of controversy and complaint I consistently received more letters in support of my explorations than against them. But a fair majority of these supportive letters came from people outside the church – some looking back wistfully but scarcely hopefully at the church, others telling me that my facing of questions came as a much-needed boost to persuade them to stay in the church.

All these reactions to me – positive as well as negative – combined to undermine my own confidence in the church as the community and source through which I had been put in the way of faith since my boyhood. Initially, I scarcely recognized this painful fact, and certainly did not come to terms with it. While I remained in office I was too busy. I was sustained by the warmth of support that I received from most of the parishes in my diocese, and the friendliness and rapport that I developed with so many people, in public positions and as private individuals, in the North East. Thus I remained fully and enthusiastically occupied with pastoral, teaching, missionary and organizational work, enjoying the wide range of stimulating invitations from all sorts of organizations, representative bodies and associations which had been prompted by the much-publicized controversies.

Thus sustained and preoccupied, I thought I had sufficiently sidelined the undermining effects of the Christian-generated attacks upon me by employing cheerful slogans. I made much use of the slogan 'Even the church cannot keep a good God down,' and frequently remarked that 'Being a bishop in the Church of England has brought me nearer to atheism than anything else in my life.' It was not until I had settled into the comparative detachment of retirement that I began to reflect systematically on how near I had actually been to atheism at times – and how near at times I remained there.

I delayed consideration of the implications of this in order to tackle what I had decided would be my first priority in retirement. I was determined to follow up the political and economic skirmishes of my controversial years in office with a sustained attempt to analyse the plausibility of the one real faith shared in our globalized present – the faith in the free market as the one and only assured means to earthly prosperity and progress for all. That book took four years to write, and was published in 2000 under the title *Market Whys and Human Wherefores*. I felt impelled to write this book because of my conviction that as a result of this common investment in the idea of the market, Christian faith, theology and witness had to come to terms with this practical and powerful idolatry if it was to re-engage with common reality.

My experiences as Bishop of Durham, however, showed me that engaging with reality as it is commonly perceived by the vast number of people in our present secularized society is the last thing that the church and the churches wish to do. Institutional Christianity in all its guises seems determined to live in the past and to draw its directions from there, from the worlds of the Old Testament, the New Testament, the early church and the patriarchal society of the mediaeval Mediterranean. Yet all these worlds are worlds apart from the interlinked and globalized earth as we now experience it. This turned-inward aspect of the churches, away from the world in the name, apparently, of traditional faith and practice, is one of the main themes of this book.

So my personal need to pursue my pilgrimage of faith and understanding by writing a book on economics delayed my getting to grips with setting out the story of where my simply believing in God landed me after I jumped enthusiastically (and, as I believe, faithfully) into being Bishop of Durham. I had assembled sheaves of notes and drafts for this book while wrestling with my book on the market. However, I did not get down to writing until the new millennium.

The symbolic significance of the beginning of a third thousand years of a Christian faith which appeared preoccupied with keeping alive minority institutions obstinately fixed on an ever more distant past for definition, sustenance and direction deepened my personal questionings about the status and scope of my own simple belief in God. I embarked on this challenge to my faith confident that, if faithfully faced, it would enlarge my belief, but still the shadow of atheism hovered around and threatened to deepen.

The task of writing this book therefore emerged as the next stage in my personal discipleship and the development of the ministry of my calling. The job I had embraced as an unexpected and exciting climax to my pilgrimage of faith had thrown up the most profound challenge to that faith I had ever encountered in my life.

Autobiographically, therefore, I start to discuss my life of faith from what is bound to be one of its last stages – my becoming Bishop of Durham. The story details how my simply believing in God fared when I behaved as the public figure of the Bishop of Durham in a manner consistent with the belief of my life. This account is, of course, written with hindsight, and designed to throw into relief how disturbed I became by what seemed to me to be the increasing evidence of how limited a faith about God, and how unrealistic an understanding of the world, underpinned the defence thrown up against me by my sincerely faithful opponents.

My readers will have to decide whether my view of the case arises entirely out of stubborn conceit or whether there are sufficient elements of insight in it. I hope that I would not have attempted to write this book if I did not sincerely, hopefully, and indeed reasonably believe that my pilgrimage of faith had, by God's grace, given me sufficient faithful insights to balance the stubborn mistakes about the world, God and indeed myself that are part of the condition of being human. There is a sense in which that 'always remains to be seen'. I take as my personal encouragement for hope and perseverance the down-to-earth comment of Paul the apostle about love (tucked significantly away at the end of the marvellous chapter in his first letter to the Corinthians): 'For now we see through a glass darkly [Greek 'riddle-wise'] but then face to face: then shall I know even as I am known' (1 Corinthians 13.12). In writing this book, therefore, I am hoping to clarify something for myself by attempting to lay it out for others.

The title of this introduction is: 'Is it a Mistake to Take God for Granted?' There is no doubt that I *have* taken God for granted since my teens and through my adult life so far. It has become increasingly obvious to me over the years of my retirement that this was a questionable perspective on life. This recognition has led me to examine how my questioning of this stance arose out of my experiences of ten years as a bishop. In the last chapter, 'Going On with God', I have tried to set out as clearly as I can what I now see as the promises, possibilities and demands of believing in God for the new millennium. My pilgrimage has led me back to a re-statement of my simply believing in God – hopefully enlarged and reformed by my experience of facing, as honestly as I can, the serious possibility that there is no God and that my simply taking God for granted is a mistake.

As far as I can see, it is impossible to claim that this decision of mine to go on accepting the reality of what I know in faith is a 'rational' decision in the narrow sense of that term prevalent in these modern and postmodern times. That is to say, I can see no way whatever of *proving* the existence of God to everyone of reasonable intelligence and goodwill. I cannot *prove* this with any reasons that would be commonly accepted as universally valid and conclusive. Indeed, to my mind, if there were such a set of arguments, accepted by most thinking people as proving the existence of God, atheism would be formally and finally established – for this could only demonstrate that 'God' was a human construction. Either there is the 'more than us', the transcendent God who has to establish his or her or its being and presence in his or her or its own way, or we are the only emergent questioning and wondering beings in the universe as we know it so far. We seek to 'reach out' beyond ourselves – but there is always the possibility that we reach out to nothing. At the latest assessment, 'physics tells us' that everything starts from a void of energy (or from the energy of the void) and either ends that way or is endlessly recycled. There is the possibility that that is all there is – whatever the mysteries, excitements or miseries we may conjure up for ourselves in the minuscule nano-moment of space-time in which we experience ourselves as existing.

I do not believe this. I have decided that I can continue simply to believe in God. This is my story and I am sticking to it. So this book is a continuation of the argument of my life – informed by a developing and questioning faith in the God who is, I believe, the life of my argument. My continuing argument, therefore, is designed to confirm and develop my faith and, it may be, to help to confirm and inspire the faith of fellow believers. At the same time, I hope that I may be drawing the attention of might-be believers, or certainly would-not-be believers, to the riches for our shared humanity encompassed in the possibilities of the glory and love of God. Above all, I have tried to set out a protest to the church at large (and not least the Church of England) about the ways in which too much of current Christian faith, practice and preaching is turned inwards into 'religion'. We are trapping God in a religion that is shaped by the past and ignores the future, a religion that simply overlooks the real world as we now see it to exist.

I am haunted by the exasperated comment made by a bishop of the Syrian Orthodox Church from Kerala. We were attending a large ecumenical gathering dedicated to the concerns of church and society. In frustration, the bishop stood up to denounce one session, picturing his fellow-delegates as a group of faithful sheep turning inwards in a closed circle, 'wriggling their tails at the world while bleating down one another's noses and claiming that this was the breath of the Spirit'.

If there is a real living and loving God, then however much the practice of religion may turn inwards, surely the pursuit of the promise of a lively faith must be turned outwards into the world as it is now.

My experiences have brought me to the point where it is not

enough for me to respond to each new challenge to faith in God by holding that, nonetheless, I simply continue to believe. I have to render an account to myself (and indeed to others). Through this autobiographical self-examination I have justified to myself the decision of my own mind and heart that I will not be drawn any further into atheism – however challenging the possibility of atheism is in view of our present experience and observation of the realities of our world, our human history and ourselves. This is the account of why I remain convinced that I may continue to rely on the gift of believing in God.

1 Belief in God and what it is to be human

What resources are available to us for developing our living selves and our shared humanity? Do we have any shared prospects and is there any lasting promise in them?

It is my conviction that human beings need urgently to rediscover that 'God' is not the invented concern of social networks in response to psychological needs labelled 'religious', but the dynamic, challenging and promising resource of all life when it reaches the level and mystery of persons. God, freed once again from his inverted commas, promises the human animals who have emerged as persons all the difference in the world – and beyond.

This understanding of, and hope in, God presents drastic challenges to the Christian churches if we are to measure up to our twenty-first-century world and our proclaimed belief in the eternal God who is deeply engaged in the processes and possibilities of ourselves and the world.

I had drafted my introduction and sketched out the first chapters of this book when the world literally and metaphorically blew up in our Western faces in the attack on the United States of 11 September 2001. It had seemed to me pretty obvious for some time that the pressures of capitalist economics, of competing value-systems and incompatible expectations in our shrinking globalized world were building up to something highly critical and probably explosive. But

1

I had no inkling that religions and faiths would be so directly and wretchedly bound up with the form that that explosion took. The destruction wrought by the hijacked planes on the twin towers of the World Trade Centre in New York and at the Pentagon in Washington was rigorously planned and ruthlessly carried out by people prepared to die for what they claimed to be a divine mission. This devastating and highly symbolic attack on the USA was launched as part of the violent protest against American domination of the world and that society's exploitation of developing countries – in particular Arab and other Islamic states from the Middle East through Central Asia to Indonesia. American organization of a counter-attack against the Taliban regime in Afghanistan as the base for and protector of the terrorist organization responsible for the September attacks fuelled and magnified the rallying cry for a *jihad*, a holy war in defence of the Muslim faith worldwide in face of Western aggressors, white oppressors who are, by definition, Christian. The readiness – even enthusiasm – for advancing the war, so defined, through suicide bombers who volunteer for death as the supreme service to Allah rests on a belief endorsed and fed by a religious faith that a martyr's death is a direct and irrefutable passport to heaven.

I am not directly concerned here with the geopolitical, economic and nationalistic ramifications of all this. My concern is the stark fact that religious faiths are deeply compromised by these events. We only have to look at the desperately miserable situation in which the Jewish and Palestinian Arab communities are locked, in and around the state of Israel. Whatever the rights and wrongs, from whatever perspective or point of view, it is clear that religious faith bears significant responsibility for the creation of the modern Jewish state in Palestine. The claims of the Jews (of the people of Israel) to a stake, and hence a state, in the 'Promised Land' have roots running back three thousand years or more. It was God, it is alleged, who gave Jerusalem and its territories to Israel in the time of Moses and Joshua. The absolute right of all Jews to have access to the Temple Mount in the modern city of Jerusalem lies in that divine gift. I have heard this belief stated clearly and simply since 11 September 2001 by a highly articulate Western-educated Israeli diplomat. The Jewish claim to divine gift, to divine right, is practical politics.

But being a Western Christian, how can I proffer easy self-righteous criticism of Jewish behaviour in the 'Holy Land' or any ill-considered criticism of the existence of Israel? The case for a homeland of their own for the Jews in modern times was promoted by the Christian West out of guilt for what persistent anti-semitism in the Christian church and among self-professed Christian states had perpetrated against the Jews. The dreadful irony is that now that there is a Jewish state, the Jews have proved to be as ready as any other nation state to exploit their territory and to expand it at the expense of others – in this case, the Palestinian Arabs. This conflict in Palestine/Israel, combined with the strong support of Israel by the USA, has served as a focusing provocation and justification for the attack on the great capitalist 'Shaitan' by fanatics and terrorists – or holy warriors for Islam, as they conceive themselves. Thus the circle is closed. All three theistic religions of revelation (Judaism, Christianity and Islam) are locked in a conflict which threatens what stability, peace and progress in human life there are on this earth.

This striking example of religious faith acting as the catalyst of conflict and destruction throws into sharp relief the harm that theistic belief in a revelatory God of power and promise has done for centuries, if not millennia. The expansion of the Christian powers of Europe from the end of the fifteenth century onwards, born of trading and missionary activity, brought misery and exploitation to the Americas, to Africa, to the Indian subcontinent, and to South Asia and the East Indies. In Christianity's own European and Mediterranean heartlands, where Christianity was adopted as the official religion of society, civilization and the state, the church authorities repeatedly abused their power with inquisitions and persecutions in defence of their self-declared orthodoxy. Wars over whose version of belief should be acceptable and imposed became endemic.

The terrorist events of 11 September 2001 and their aftermath embody the harm that theistic belief is used to justify. They remind the whole world of the way the patriarchal authorities of the theistic faiths – whether mitred, turbaned or skullcapped – vociferously proclaim their possession of definitive truths of faith in the one, true and only God in contradiction to one another, each using their own certainty to exonerate themselves from personal responsibility for the evil perpetrated in crusades, *jihads* and persecutions across the world.

The events of 11 September underline a conclusion that seems increasingly obvious. The principal and decisive reason for not believing in God is the behaviour of the people who yell that they do.

To a person like me, who simply believes in God, and remains clear that this is a reasonable and hopeful way of life, this is particularly disturbing and destructive. My experience is that the case for believing in God comes alive precisely in the company of a community or set of communities where people work at developing their belief.

In other words, belief in God depends for its initiation and sustenance on people who are already conscious of their belief in God – and yet, as a collective class, people who make such admissions are the principal obstacles to believing in God. This is the paradox of the church.

This book is written as a sustained attempt to live with that paradox. But the question remains whether the paradox is so severe as to be in effect a contradiction. Does the past history and present behaviour of the church and churches prove to any reasonable person of moderate insight and decent good will that God cannot and should not be believed in? A thread of heartfelt complaint running through this book arises from my experience that very few among either the church authorities or enthusiastic members of congregations display any realistic awareness of this negative face of church life. Too much of church life, talk and worship seems to me to have shrunk into religious practices which can attract and hold only persons who are already hopelessly 'religious', rather than the faithfully hopeful who are turned outwards towards the world and God.

11 September 2001 forced me to review my reflections on my experiences, the arguments I had developed in my coming to grips with those experiences, and the working assumptions under which I was composing this book and the faith in which I was continuing my pilgrimage of belief. Presented with the closed faces and rhetoric of hatred of these 'warriors of God', surely the rational response has to be that there is no God. The practices of faith (and faiths) involve too much dangerous and destructive nonsense. The phrase of that eighteenth-century rationalist, libertarian and deist, Voltaire, rings out across time. Faced with the excesses and follies of official religion in France, he exclaimed, '*Écrasez l'infame*' – scrub out such infernal rubbish.

The protest seems to me all too often justified, and yet I continue to believe in God. I do not believe that it is appropriate, humane or realistic to respond to the at times agonizing problem of what people claim to be licensed to do by their belief in God by rejecting all ideas of a transcendent possibility or of a revelation from a spiritual resource beyond ourselves.

Two independent, though connected, lines of argument lead me to this decision. The first is that the case for atheism is by no means as obvious or decisive as atheistic humanists, scientific reductionists and pragmatic down-to-earthers like to think. The dominant mind-set, at least in the West, assumed that there is no God. As Laplace said at the beginning of the nineteenth century, 'We have found no need for that hypothesis.' For the most part, the enthusiastic and devoted proponents of the theistic religions are completely unready to face this. I found this to be so among many of the Christians who joined in the arguments about my views. They were only interested in arguing over whether I was truly 'faithful' by their lights, oblivious to the fact that to the wider public such debates were irrelevant because they could see no God at all.

To my mind, the petty prejudices displayed by religious people about beliefs, morals and actions are a far stronger obstacle to reviving widespread belief in a living God than are the more metaphysical, logical and philosophical arguments claiming to demonstrate the impossibility of the existence of God. Still, given the way so many people urging divine revelation and spiritual guidance display their belief, I cannot see the adoption of atheism as either blameworthy or irresponsible. The real question is whether atheism, rigorously adopted and applied, is a necessary, sufficient and worthy approach to the most amazing existence so far known to us to have emerged in this universe. Human beings, it seems to me, are a mystery worthy of further investigation and reflection.

The second line of reflection that supports me in persisting with my decision to go on holding and responding to my decision to continue pursuing my simple belief in God was distilled for me when, faced by the horrors of 11 September 2001, I was considering whether I could or should go on writing this book – and if so, how.

It dawned on me that now we human beings are back to normal. When the Berlin Wall was dismantled in 1989 we were tempted by the image to believe that it marked the end of serious enmities between world powers espousing different systems and ideologies. Now the way was clear for the steady growth in productivity, prosperity and general human progress in the march towards universal democracy and liberal freedoms. With the free market powering progress, the whole world would move towards increasing affluence with only the occasional interruption. We would be able to deal with any little blips that came up by means of our increasingly sophisticated manipulations, or by discovering some technological fix. War was confined to tribal affairs in Third World countries or fringe states in Eastern Europe and the Middle East. The development of prosperity would eventually cure such ills. Naturally prosperity would not come until these countries had organized modern governmental structures that dealt with the problems of endemic corruption, but once such advances had been made, the benighted Third World would be fit to plug into the global economy. International corporations would move in and democracy and prosperity would flow forward together. Of course the process would take time, but the conventional hope in the West was that the necessary economic and political processes were free to work their magic.

This was nonsense, of course. The failure of the hopes of 'a world fit for heroes' for which my father and his comrades fought the First World War and the dreams I and those demobbed with me invested in Beveridge plans and the postwar government's plans for a welfare state after the Second World War demonstrated that there is no magic formula, no golden rule, that ensures enduring progress for ever more human beings, however much you wish there were. Human society must always wrestle with its present reality – judging what actions and consequences are necessary, rather than acquiescing in existing processes simply because they are there.

This brings us back to the question whether there are resources available beyond ourselves with which we, as self-conscious, thinking and longing human beings, are capable of co-operating for good. Are we really on our own?

These reflections brought me back to the first stage of my verging on atheism rather than forcing me on into an atheistic conclusion. They reminded me that the stories told in the tradition about the reality of believing in God, the prayers and psalms recorded by faith in the Bible (in both the Old and the New Testaments), hardly reflect certainty and complacent serenity as typical features of the experience of believing in God. Those labelled the 'people of God' in the Bible are neither regularly obedient to God nor blameless examples of faith in God. From the third chapter of the Old Testament onwards, God starts having trouble with men and women, trouble that carries on throughout the Bible, save in a few visions of 'the End'. Yet the stylized creation myth with which the Bible begins makes the confident statement: 'And God saw everything that he had made and behold it was very good' (Genesis 1.31).

Archaeologists continue to add to the range of inscriptions that throw light on the early myths prevalent in the Near East and there are parallels to the Genesis story. But I do not think there is any precise parallel to this serene affirmation of the overarching good of the process that has produced the earth and us. Of course this is an insight and hope of faith expressed in mythological terms. I will develop later how I see the application of it to us human beings locked in 'the absolutely minuscule nano-moment of space-time' in which we experience ourselves as existing. My purpose now is to draw attention to the way in which the Bible opens hopefully, then goes on with a catalogue of tales of disaster, disobedience and despair – but through them all runs this golden thread of prophetic voices denouncing what goes wrong and contrasting its insufficiency in the light of the promise and hope of God's future. That prophetic strand of hope, that hope lived out in the life, death and resurrection of Jesus, is the very heart of the experiences of faith which are both the basis and the dynamic of Christian 'simply believing in God'.

This is a major theme in the wrestlings of this book. I mention it here to point up why my reflection that 11 September 2001 returned human history to normality liberated me from the notion that the evidence of the behaviour of adherents to the three theistic faiths claiming revelation from God pushed me ever nearer to atheism.

On a different scale, the issue of the argument against the faith provided by its vociferous adherents was precisely what I had been forced to face during my experience as Bishop of Durham. So on reflection, 11 September 2001 did not therefore present me with a new challenge to embrace atheism. I could get on with this book as planned as a vehicle for my own coming to terms with the realities of Christian believing in the context of the twenty-first century. It was clear to me, however, that I did need to sharpen up my recognition of the difficulties involved. I am firm in my conviction that a faith that cannot look directly at the independent realities of this world and ourselves is a bromide, a mere escape, and not a revelation and a hope. I can best explain what I mean here with an autobiographical illustration.

From 1969 to 1973 I settled with my wife and younger children in Geneva while I served on the staff of the World Council of Churches as 'Director of Humanum Studies'. This post was created as a result of the Conference of the World Council of Churches held in Uppsala in Sweden in 1968. The Director had no department. As an independent theologian he was expected to pick up critical issues from the various departments of the Council (departments such as those for Faith and Order and for Church and Society; the Churches Council for International Affairs and the department for World Mission and Evangelism). The title of 'Director of Humanum Studies' came out of a conviction that the central issue for the churches in the fourth quarter of the twentieth century was Christian anthropology. Since beings are concerned with human being and becoming, where does God as revealed in Jesus through the Spirit come in?

Although it remained a congenial existence, I had begun to find the life of a theology don at Oxford a bit claustrophobic. So I welcomed this opportunity. With the enthusiastic support of my wife, we packed up and migrated to Geneva with our two youngest children for four years. My erstwhile colleagues were somewhat startled by the move. Some friendly well-wishers informed me privately that I had departed just as I was in the running for three different senior posts in or around Oxford. The general conclusion was that I had probably scuppered my career.

My time with the World Council of Churches broadened my understanding of the scope of the gospel. It convinced me of the priority that should be given to social and economic problems in the governance of the world (not least in the Third World) and gave me rich experience of the bewildering variety of forms of Christianity, of human culture and lifestyles around the globe.

The job led me to participate in some highly interesting international theological and interdisciplinary sessions at the Ecumenical Institute at Bossey, on the shores of Lake Geneva. One session was concerned with psychiatry, sociology and theology and their practical implications for the care of the sick. One day I felt that we had been cursed with too much theological waffle (matched, I fear, by some psychological and sociological waffle). So I escaped after dinner for a walk by the lake. My companion was a small bearded man, a sociologist from the Netherlands. He declared himself an atheist. (I frequently found that I got on better with atheists in this type of discussion than with many fellow Christians.) For some reason or other, as we stopped under some trees, I remember remarking, 'I want to get at the truth, you see.' My companion looked me straight in the eye and replied, 'Yes, I believe you do. Nobody will thank you.' That exchange has stayed with me as a remarkable encouragement and challenge.

Looking back several decades on, I can now see that I was not as brave or as bold as all that. I was simply believing in God, so I already 'knew' that the risks were worth taking. But to be consistent, one must take risks to the very end. So I have gone on to write this book as originally planned, with I hope the benefit of a deeper recognition of the true nature of the challenge.

A final word on the title, *The Calling of a Cuckoo*. The phrase is drawn from a couple of lines in a speech given by Mrs Thatcher when she was Prime Minister and leader of the Conservative Party. She was addressing a meeting of the Conservative Central Council in Newcastle on Saturday 28 March 1985, when I had been in office barely nine months. As the *Sunday Express* reported under the headline 'Maggie Blasts Cuckoo Bishops', she said:

> You may have noticed that recently the voices of some reverend and right-reverend prelates have been heard in the land. I make no complaint about that. After all, it wouldn't be spring, would it, without the voice of the occasional cuckoo!

While there was no specific reference to me, commentators seemed eager to read it that way. When I came to write this book, it seemed to provide me with a suitable – and not too solemn – title for it. On reflection it occurred to me that there was more to it than that. The notion that a Prime Minister should voice a public dismissal of my views showed that I had managed to engage in political and economic realities in ways that had caught her attention, even if they had not ruffled her assumptions. This book is an investigation of God the Disturber in regard to troubling matters of faith and life, of politics and economics. *The Calling of a Cuckoo* therefore seems an appropriate title – besides which, there are always the interesting implications of being a cuckoo in the nest.

2 'God the disturber'

On the morning of Monday 27 February 1984, I made my usual weekday journey into the office I occupied in the red-brick terraced house that accommodates the Department of Theology and Religious Studies at the University of Leeds. I was beginning my fifth year as Professor of Theology and Head of Department there, having come to the university in January 1979. I had celebrated my fifty-ninth birthday the previous month, so, as far as I knew, I was well into the middle of my last job before retirement.

I was, by and large, very happy at Leeds. The Department was friendly and I greatly enjoyed teaching. The professor's job included giving a course of lectures on the nature and scope of Christian theology for first-year honours students from the Arts Faculty. All first-year honours arts students were required to take a course in a third subject. A good number each year signed up for theology, some because of a curiosity about that 'stuff about the Bible', others on the assumption that it would be a comparatively easy option. The challenge of these lectures was sharpened by my discovery that the majority of my audience were unlikely to pick up references to either the Bible or to Gilbert and Sullivan. Fortunately, over the years I have developed a strong sense of humour. (I am not sure where this came from, for my father was rather solemn, and looking back I now realize that my mother, who was a dear, was inclined to be depressive.) I surmounted the challenge of communication, and attendance at the lectures kept up.

In the university at large I got on very well with most colleagues, whether bureaucratic or academic. I served as Dean of Arts for two years and became the sort of person nominated for tiresome administrative jobs, such as representing the Faculty of Arts on promotion committees – the committees responsible for maintaining equable and fair promotions across the faculties. (Philosophical reflection on the implications and requirements for this would, of course, have inhibited any action – so we just got on with the job.) When I first took my plunge into university affairs beyond the strict exercise of my role as theology professor, I was much encouraged by a friendly professor sitting next to me at my first staff dinner. If I remember rightly, he came from the engineering faculty. He told me cheerfully that he presumed I knew that I had been appointed Professor of Theology not *because* I was a priest and a Canon Theologian of Leicester but *despite* these facts. He was thus defending the founding tradition of the University of Leeds as a secular and businesslike establishment. It was clear both from his body language and the way he made his point that this was intended as a friendly and welcoming observation. I was quite prepared to meet the challenge with equal friendliness and enthusiasm.

I was, therefore, well esconced. There was some gossip that the next time a Pro-Vice-Chancellor was required for the Arts side of the university I might be considered a serious candidate. I have never been afraid of administration, since I had been broken into it at an early age as a young staff officer in GHQ in India at the end of the Second World War. When I was a Fellow of The Queen's College, Oxford, I had served as Domestic Bursar during a time when the college was thrown into disarray by a crisis in the running of its kitchens. Our Provost at the time, Lord Florey, then a recent past President of the Royal Society, persuaded me to take the job with an outrageous piece of flattery (the nature of which both he and I were well aware). He wanted me for the job, he said, because I was 'the only member of the Governing Body with a scientific approach to things'. I found a certain satisfaction in carrying out administration as efficiently as possible within and for my Department.

The prospect of a 'call to higher service' in the university merely hovered as a vague possibility for the future. I had no desire or need to seek additional occupations. From previous appointments at Oxford University and working in Geneva for four years on the World Council of Churches I had acquired a network of contacts among people and institutions that fed me with more than sufficient opportunities for pursuing a variety of subjects among bodies and interest-groups around the world. I had been visiting the United States and Canada regularly since 1968. (My first invitation to the States resulted in my finding myself preaching the three-hour Good Friday service at Trinity Church, Wall Street, in New York just a few days after the assassination of Martin Luther King.) I was on a Medical Missionary and World Health Organization network that involved me in the discussion of NHS issues at home and took me to conferences in Geneva, at the German Institute for Medical Mission in Tübingen and elsewhere. I had contacts in Australia, where I had my first lecture tour in 1972. Back at home I was engaged in Church of England affairs centring on issues of theological education, social matters and ecumenical developments. I was regularly invited to preach, to give talks and to participate in consultations not only in my local parish and diocese but across the country, and by other denominations as well as my own. All these were opportunities which I expected would extend into my retirement. In short, at the beginning of 1984 I had plenty to occupy myself with and plenty to look forward to.

So I entered my room in the Department shortly after nine that Monday 27 February with nothing but routine matters on my mind. I had a philosophy of religion class at noon and I was ready for that. As soon as I had greeted the staff in the departmental office, Ingrid, our very efficient departmental secretary, brought in the mail. As usual it was quite a pile, topped by a large brown envelope of the type that suggested a request from somewhere in the university bureaucracy (probably the Bursar) for some no doubt highly useful piece of information. It was indeed from the Bursar and I promptly passed it on to Ingrid, to whom such things were child's play. The removal of that first piece of mail revealed two long white envelopes of suspiciously high quality stuck in the pile. The top one was upside-down and I saw the address '10 Downing Street' embossed on the back. Instinctively, I opened the middle drawer of my desk, slipped the two envelopes inside and closed the drawer. Neither Ingrid nor I made any comment, and we proceeded to deal with the rest of the mail.

When Ingrid went off to deal with the correspondence I got out the letters and opened them. They were both dated 23 February 1984 and had been delayed by the weekend. One was signed by Mrs Thatcher, as Prime Minister. It asked me whether I would be willing for her to submit my name to the Queen for appointment to the vacant See of Durham. The other was from the Secretary for Appointments at Downing Street offering his help and advice on various consequential matters.

As soon as I set eyes on the envelopes I had realized what they must contain. Therefore in some sense or other I must have had an awareness of the possibility of their arrival. Yet I had begun that day with nothing but routine matters on my mind.

The inconsistency here is heightened by what I said to my wife, Mollie. I picked up the phone and called her at the pair of houses in downtown Leeds which she had developed as a day centre for some dozen 'drop-out' teenagers. She had named the project 'Caravanserai': it was a temporary protected lodging for these boys and girls, who had been referred to her by various local authorities or social workers. She was deeply and personally involved in her enterprise and, like me, she was not looking for, nor expecting, a move. Nonetheless, when she came on the telephone I simply said, 'The letter's come.' She understood at once what I meant and responded with a suitable expletive. After a brief conversation we agreed to get on with what we were doing and leave further discussion until we arrived home that evening. I was later informed by a surprised colleague of hers that she had retired to the woodworking room in the basement and had planed a substantial piece of wood nearly to destruction without a word of explanation. I, meanwhile, took my philosophy of religion class and spent the afternoon on a committee discussing the purchase of theological books at the Central University Library.

If the mere sight of the 10 Downing Street address convinced me that I was being offered a bishopric, and if my wife immediately understood the reference to 'the letter' as such, how can I now be honest when I introduce my account of this life-changing day in our lives by emphasizing how settled Mollie and I were and how little we expected any change? The answer is that it had occurred to me back in 1983 when the then Bishop of Durham was elevated to the Archbishopric of York that I might be a candidate as his successor. The months had passed, however, and I had come to the grateful conclusion that I was not in danger.

I highlight my attitude at the time because I can now see that it played a big part in the way I handled (or mishandled) the opportunities that opened to me when the invitation to be Bishop of Durham turned up. The truth is that I did not want to be a bishop in the Church of England, though that church was the context and community through which I was working out my vocation to be a Christian disciple, priest and missionary. I had made this fact as clear as I could in the informal, gossipy way in which messages were passed on to 'the powers-that-be' in the Church of England at that time. (Nobody, then, ever applied for a bishopric; no one ever had a serious career discussion with anyone in any sort of authority about such mysteries.) I recollect the incidental remark of an archbishop during the 1970s that he thought I should join the bench of bishops, another indication from a diocesan bishop that he would be happy to have me as an episcopal colleague, and one enquiry from a senior clergyman in a diocese who was speaking, as he said, on behalf of a group of fellow clergy who wanted to know if I would be prepared to have them put my name forward as their contribution to the routine consultations that were taking place. On all these occasions I had indicated my lack of interest.

I had never seen the point of my becoming a bishop. For me the weight of episcopal office meant being sucked into largely church-centred activities. From the earliest days of my pursuit of my calling as a priest I saw myself as an operator on the frontiers between the church and the world at large, between institutional Christianity and the organizations of society, intellectual, political and economic. I was clear that the church – that continuing community of believers, worshippers and pilgrims – was essential to sustaining and serving Christian faith. But the church was not the kingdom of God. It was the principal witness to the existence and promise of that kingdom and a major – although by no means exclusive or always discerning – servant of that kingdom. In short, I had never assumed a bishopric necessarily to be some sort of climax to a Christian calling and a priestly ministry.

When I drove home that night after receiving the Downing Street letters I 'felt' – for that is the best word I can come up with to describe my rather vague thoughts – that Mollie and I would reply negatively to the Prime Minister's invitation. My wife was deeply committed to Caravanserai and, as I have indicated, I was enjoying my professorship at Leeds. When I had responded negatively to the previous soundings, Mollie had been much relieved. In view of the mixture of sense of duty, great enthusiasm and conceited lack of self-knowledge in my make-up, she feared that in a bishopric I would soon run the risk of giving myself a breakdown, or something worse. Hence my vaguely formed expectation as I drove home was that the Downing Street letters would prove to be nothing but a brief, if flattering, disturbance.

To my surprise, my wife's reaction was quite different from what I had expected. What she said to me when we met that Monday evening is recorded – almost verbatim as I remember it – in an interview she gave to a women's magazine for its Christmas number later that year.

> It was a difficult decision to accept the job. We had a very pleasant life indeed – our own house, lots of friends, work he really enjoyed, and we saw a lot of each other; and then this lot comes. You cannot say no if you have fought for the Church of England all your life. I told him that he had always preached about 'God the Disturber' and he could hardly say that he himself wasn't going to be disturbed – but he accepted it with a deep sigh, quite honestly.

So that was that. I particularly remember my wife's additional phrase about my not being able to forget the idea of God the

Disturber just because I was in my sixtieth year. My reply to the Prime Minister had to be positive.

There is, of course, the possibility that although I believe that my story as I have just related it is true, my imagination has modified it to conform to the traditional role of a devout servant of the Lord acting with proper humility in face of an offer of a prestigious appointment. The Bishopric of Durham is the fourth most senior post in the Church of England hierarchy. In the mid-1980s it carried with it a seat in the House of Lords. I am confident, however, that I am not complying with this pious myth. I am trying to be as clear as possible, in retrospect, about my motives, hopes and expectations when faced with becoming a bishop in the Church of England after fifty years of simply believing in God.

My account of the twenty-four hours in which my wife and I decided that I had to be ready to become the Bishop of Durham demonstrates that my decision blended a good deal of assurance about God with a distinct ambivalence about the Church of England. It was a combination that was soon to produce volatile, if not explosive, results.

The next day I made an appointment to see the Vice-Chancellor to inform him of my decision to make a move. Mollie wrote as follows to our elder daughter Deborah, who was at that time in Hungary on a British Council scholarship.

> It has happened! The dreaded letter from Downing Street arrived a few days ago[1] and it looks as though we shall have to go to Durham in the autumn. We have very mixed feelings about it but we feel we can't – shouldn't – refuse.

---

1 In fact we had seen it only the day before, but my wife was assuming that her letter would take several days to reach Hungary.

A week then passed during which I interspersed my regular engagements with such things as a medical check-up. (As Mollie wrote to our daughter, 'They don't want him to drop dead in the job.') On Ash Wednesday (7 March 1984) I travelled down to London to see the Appointments Secretary at 10 Downing Street carrying a brief letter to the Prime Minister that I intended to hand over to the Secretary if one or two questions about future arrangements were answered satisfactorily. They were, and the letter was duly handed over. In it I wrote:

> I trust that my sending you this letter on Ash Wednesday does not indicate that my wife and I have entered on too penitential a way of life – and I thank you for the honour you have done me.

My appointment as Bishop of Durham was announced a week later on 14 March. Because of the seniority of my appointment it was widely reported, but without much comment. After all, there was not much to be said. I had prospered academically and gone down reasonably well in my pastoral work during fifteen years at Oxford. In 1966 I had delivered a series of Bampton Lectures – an established and respected lectureship in theological circles, which was published in 1967 as *The Glory of Man*. That year a paperback of mine was also published, entitled *A Guide to the Debate about God*; it went through five impressions in three years and was well received as a contribution to the defence and exposition of orthodox Christian belief at the time of the 1960s debates. In 1969 my wife and I, along with our two daughters, left England for Geneva and a period of travel that I believe we all enjoyed. Both personally and professionally it greatly expanded my experience. In the circles in which I was known I was reported to have a reputation for interest in scholarship, lively involvement in social affairs, and orthodox Christian faith. This reputation was not, of course, widespread. So my appointment was met with a faint air of surprise in the wider world. My own local press in Leeds, and the press in Durham where I was to go, were welcoming and encouraging, as was the *Church Times*. In the national press comments were limited and routine. I appeared to be attaining the summit of respectability as the fourth most senior prelate in the Church of England after a varied, valid and fairly useful academic and pastoral career as a priest.

That is not how it all turned out.

3 TV and the beginning of notoriety

Within a mere seven weeks of the announcement of my appointment as Bishop of Durham I had been precipitated from locally recognized respectability into generally publicized notoriety. This is how it came about.

During March and April 1984 (running up to Easter Day, 22 April), London Weekend Television broadcast a miniseries on 'Jesus, the Evidence' as part of their *Credo* programme. *Credo* was LWT's contribution to the 'God slot', a protected period on Sunday reserved for religious television broadcasting. It fitted into the tradition still lingering on from the days when a thriving Religious Affairs Department at the BBC had provided regular programmes on radio and television devoted to discussion of the proper observance of the Christian seasons and decent explorations of religious faith, morals and social affairs. The tradition had been set when the BBC was formed in the 1920s under its first Director-General, Lord Reith. A staunch Presbyterian, Lord Reith was determined that a British public broadcasting corporation should make regular provision for Christian faith and Christian affairs in and for a Christian country. The tradition of religious broadcasting as part of a station's output had been weakening from the 1950s onwards, but in the early 1980s the 'God slot' remained in the weekend scheduling on radio and television. However, although it was protected by law, the God slot was under siege and, feeling the pressure to bolster declining ratings, religious producers were inclining towards more controversial and sensationalist presentations of religious topics.

For their 'Jesus, the Evidence' series the *Credo* producers assembled a collection of biblical scholars, theologians and interested lay people from both inside and outside the churches to explain and discuss the impact of modern critical study of the four Gospels and how advances in knowledge affected understanding of Jesus. Most of the ideas discussed in the programmes were not in fact all that 'modern'. Ever since the nineteenth century scholars have debated a whole series of questions about the historical and evidential value of the 'scriptures'. By the time I began my undergraduate studies in 1947, modern critical methods of studying the Bible and the developments of Christian belief and doctrine over the centuries had become commonplace in all theology faculties, and were known – if not always accepted – in the theological colleges of both the Church of England and the non-conformist denominations. I had begun to familiarize myself with the principal arguments while in the fifth form at school as I widened my reading on Christian faith and theology. So there was nothing new in the discussions broadcast in 'Jesus, the Evidence'.

What was new was the programme's approach, taking time to set such extended and systematic discussion of the impact of critical scholarship on the understanding of the scriptures before a wider public. It could also be said that the programme was structured to be 'controversial', not necessarily in order to 'make trouble' but rather as a way of defining the critical issues as clearly as possible and in as stimulating a way as possible. Non-believing commentators were used to draw attention to the way modern discoveries challenged the historical veracity of the Gospels. Commentators from both sides then debated how far these discoveries undermined the authority of the scriptures as sources of revelation about Jesus. Many viewers were unsettled by the fact that the Christian commentators who responded by stating what the Gospels meant to them contributed very different accounts of how they interpreted those Gospels and applied them to Christian belief.

The producers planned a final programme, to be broadcast on the Sunday after Easter, which would sum up the series in interviews with a range of scholars in which each would be invited to give their personal views on how the Christian faith was affected by the critical questions raised by modern scholarship. The issues were:

1. Is it possible (or should it be possible) to believe today that Jesus is 'God with us'?
2. What today should we make of the stories about miracles?
3. In particular, what should we make of the two crucial miracle stories: the virgin birth and the resurrection?

Most of the series had been recorded by the second week in March and the producers were looking to finalize the contributors to this last programme when my appointment to the Bishopric of Durham became public on 14 March.

I have been told (by gossip from 'informed sources', as is usual in the Church of England) that the producers rang Lambeth Palace seeking a recommendation for a bishop to appear on the programme. It is said that my name was mentioned as a bishop-designate who was sufficiently informed and a good preacher of balanced and orthodox views. At any rate, I was approached (as far as I was concerned, out of the blue – I had no conversation with the archbishop's office on the matter) and was asked if I was willing to be interviewed for the programme.

I should like to point out here, for future reference, that I certainly thought of myself as an informed preacher of 'balanced and orthodox views', and I still do. In support of the contention that I am not alone in this self-assessment, I would point to two statements made during the initial controversies over my views. In rejecting a petition against my being consecrated a bishop, the Archbishop of York wrote, for example:

> If the petition implies that his sincerity in making these declarations [of faith] is in doubt, then so serious a charge would need to be backed by evidence from his writings and other well-considered expressions of his belief. I note that none of those who have written to me, or have in other ways complained about his appointment, have made any derogatory references to his numerous published works. Nor have his critics shown evidence of having acquainted themselves with his thought as a whole.

Secondly, my old tutor – Dennis Nineham – a professor of theology both in London and in Bristol, and sometime Regius Professor of Divinity at Cambridge, himself well known as a New Testament scholar, took the time to point out in his sermon at my enthronement in July 1984:

> And here I should like to make it very clear that among his theological colleagues he has a high reputation as an able, honest and outspoken scholar, but not in the least as a firebrand; rather, if anything, as one who verges on the cautious and the conservative.

I suspect that Dennis Nineham may have been speaking slightly tongue-in-cheek, but I have long been aware that my friend thought

I believed a good deal more 'orthodox' theology than he did.

Looking back on the events in which I was involved in April 1984, it is absolutely clear to me that I accepted the invitation to be interviewed in the summing-up session of 'Jesus, the Evidence' as a purely routine engagement. I had taken part in television discussions before, and this one was on an issue at the very heart of my interests – theological, priestly, missionary and personal. I saw it as an opportunity to set out, as briefly and with as great a clarity as I could muster, how we in our modern world could enter into and share the belief of the writers of the Gospels. The thought never entered my head that my change of title from professor to 'bishop-designate' should alter my approach one jot or tittle. I believed that it was personal discipleship and not the professional or institutional role that was paramount in seeking to expound and communicate the truth and the love of the God whom I believe had found me.

So on the afternoon of Tuesday 24 April 1984 I arrived at the Grosvenor House Hotel in London, where the recording was to take place, in a relaxed and interested frame of mind. At this distance, I have no detailed memory of that interview. I remember feeling at ease with the presenter, Philip Whitehead. Previously Labour MP for Derby North, he was an accomplished commentator on current affairs, with the mind to pursue a coherent line of questioning.

I enjoyed our discussion and returned home feeling that I had sketched out a good case for modern and faithful belief in Jesus as 'Emmanuel', the man who was God with us and for us. I had said that the story of the virgin birth was told once this belief in Jesus had been discovered, in order to explain the faith in Jesus as both God and man – a faith that I shared. The Gospel miracles were stories, many of them similar to miracle stories told by other cultures and faiths of other people held to be holy or special messengers from God. The Gospel miracle stories, however, were told to express the impact of Jesus' actions, words and way of life, and how these raised questions and hopes – elicited wonder – about the presence and the activity of God.

In the interview I made it quite clear that 'the resurrection' was not a single miracle. Faith in the resurrection of the crucified Jesus was kindled, then confirmed, by a series of events (such as the empty tomb story). There was a series of encounters (as recounted in the last pages of the four Gospels), the cumulative effect of which was to convince the disciples and their companions – who had seen Jesus dead and knew that he was buried – that that was not the end of him. Through the power and presence of God Jesus was alive in the sphere and realm of God, in the unique way appropriate to God. To 'believe in the resurrection' is therefore to share in the conviction of the first apostles and their companions, a conviction about the reality and the world-changing power of this man, in and through the power and the presence of God.

So I travelled home that day thinking that I had made a small contribution to my calling to open up the possibilities of orthodox Christian faith to 'people at large'.

Reviewing the turbulent events into which I was plunged so swiftly after that, I realize how crucial this issue of 'people at large' was. I took it for granted that as a bishop I would be a representative figure in the church. To me this meant that my primary audience should be 'the public' – that is, people at large. To my mind this was particularly true, given that by a historical accident I was becoming a senior bishop in an 'established' church. On my appointment as Bishop of Durham I would be presented to a seat in the House of Lords. My presence there would be symbolic of an ancient historical logic that had to do with the universality of the gospel. It seemed to me that I ought to exploit the implied opportunities of this, so long as it remained there to exploit. The interweaving of church and state might now be obsolete in terms of establishment and law, but the theological logic that the gospel is universal and inclusive remains. The gospel of God in Jesus Christ is 'the same yesterday, today and forever' (Hebrews 13.8) and it is for all. Any accidental opportunity to publicize its exciting promise to the broadest possible constituency has to be seized.

So when I took part in the 'Jesus, the Evidence' programme I did not envisage myself speaking solely to church and Christian believers. My target was a much wider audience. I hoped to challenge the church and the faithful to open up their minds and spirits to the universal scope of the gospel. I was trying to engage the reality that a majority of our neighbours do not even entertain the idea of God as a possibility. Mostly, religious people are regarded as a closed class of enthusiasts with private interests of an esoteric but not widely significant nature. I wanted to wake the church up to the need to give a greater priority to this reality. So beyond the existing faithful, in the programme I was trying to reach the type of person who was sympathetic to the possibilities of God, who was drawn to the man Jesus and conscious of the possibility that Christian morality might improve the way one lives one's life – a person who sensed the potential of a perspective that allows a transcendent meaning of human being and yet was repelled by the narrow-minded dogmatism and arbitrary authoritarianism of so much Christian discourse and behaviour.

I also carried a third category of neighbours in my mind. They were the positive unbelievers, the thoughtful atheists who settle into the habit of dismissing Christian faith and all religion as obviously unreasonable and mere superstition because of the undesirable and inhumane things perpetrated in its name. This argument of atheism has been greatly strengthened by the hideous face of religious dogma that has been so prominent in our news bulletins in recent months. The case for atheism seems so much stronger now than it did in

1984 or even when I first started to sketch out this book. And yet, the churches seem as oblivious to that fact now as they were in 1984. Christians still use up their energies arguing with one another about who is right and who is a heretic over the precise authority of the church and the proper interpretation of scripture and gospel. Meanwhile they ignore the fact that most inhabitants of the Western world today cannot even envisage the idea that God might exist. To them 'God' has ceased to be a serious possibility. Those believers who argue about God are taken seriously only for the damage that we do in the world (witness the events in Israel and Palestine as I write).

I have always considered it exciting to face the challenge of that atheistic denial. It stimulates me to expound and explore the riches of Christian faith. Testing ourselves against the limited assumptions of atheism keeps Christians focused on the common issues of humanity and its future which are of direct and constant concern to us all as human beings, whether atheist or believer.

I might add that I kept one more category of person in mind – the indifferent. Today these seem to be the largest category in our society; people who tend not to get too worked up and upset about anything much, who expect fairly little from life and also hope to avoid too much misery.

So believe it or not, my interview on 24 April 1984 for 'Jesus, the Evidence' was intended as an opening shot in a campaign about the possibilities open to human beings in the light of God as he has made himself known in Jesus, and continues to work through the Holy Spirit. The church and the faithful servants of the gospel of God in Jesus Christ needed to be challenged to face today's reality – that the wistful, the atheist and the largely indifferent constitute the majority of our neighbours. This being so, what does the church think it is doing when it focuses on disputes about the parameters of official belief and the maintenance of ecclesiastical institutions? These are displacement activities. If a church, or a religion, cannot face the world as it is, then it cannot believe in a true, living God.

Today's world is several worlds apart from the times that shaped the Old Testament, the New Testament and the development of the doctrines of the early church and on into Christendom, the mediaeval period and the origins of Protestantism. Looking backwards to these past times, clinging on to interpretations of truth and authority that were shaped by dead worlds, can only constrict the church and turn it inwards on itself.

My intention had been to make a first contribution as bishop to the calling of an apostle and evangelist for the Christian gospel by opening the possibilities of faithful believing to people living in today's society. The Christian gospel is the good news of the reality, truth and love of the God who is for good for all and for all times. It is nothing if not universal and forward-looking. I learned this from the apostle Paul. If I was to be designated by one part of God's church a formalized 'successor of the apostles', then I was committed to this forward-looking dynamic towards universality. I had to pursue it at every opportunity, not because I was good at it, but because I was called to do so.

So I took the plunge in that 'Jesus, the Evidence' interview, well aware of what I was doing and why I was doing it. But in another sense I did not know what I was doing, because I failed to anticipate the dimensions of the response. I was first dumbfounded, then deeply perplexed, by the storm of trouble I appeared to have raised. Had I been cast in the role of a 'fool for Christ's sake', or was I suffering as a fool for having followed my own conceits?

The random coincidence between the date of the announcement that I was to be Bishop of Durham and the scheduling of a television discussion gave me an alarming introduction to communication through the modern media. I soon learned that a principal disadvantage of television is that the lighting kills the twinkle in the eye. The television camera gives the illusion of familiarity without the face-to-face encounter which I have always much enjoyed in my teaching, preaching, and lecturing. I met the television interviewer's questions in the same relaxed style I would use to someone at home in a parish discussion group or in a university tutorial. Yet through the lens of the camera I was addressing people I could know nothing about.

To read the verbatim transcript of the interview for the *Credo* programme was a humbling and even somewhat frightening experience. Without the verbal punctuation provided by the pacing, intonation and gestures of living delivery, the bare sequence of typed words frequently verge on incoherence. I was greatly indebted to the professional skill of Philip Whitehead, who concluded our interview by summing up my position with great fairness:

So it seems for churchmen like the Bishop-Elect of Durham *precise dogmas* about Jesus are a thing of the past. All are open to argument, if not reinterpretation.

Within this, the main thing to understand about the disputed details of Jesus's story and of views about him is that they are all rooted in *faith*.

Accounts of his birth to a virgin and such miracles as his walking on water are expressions of the early Christians' *faith* in Jesus as the Messiah. The resurrection was not a single event, but a series of experiences on the part of his disciples and followers, linked together again by their *faith* in Jesus and the conviction that he was alive among them. And the idea that Jesus was God grew gradually among the early Christians out of their *belief* that in Jesus God had become manifest as not only transcendent but at work in the world around them.

Churchmen like Professor Jenkins stand by the idea of Jesus as God because of their *faith* nourished by personal experience of God's close involvement in the world, of which they see Jesus as the ultimate revelation.

However; instead of casting out those who regard Jesus not as God but as a mortal human being acting as God's agent, churchmen like the Bishop-Elect of Durham are prepared to welcome them as Christians. And that is a big change indeed for the Church of England.

I found this a just and clear summary of the issues that I was seeking to open out.

The reception of what I said (and possibly the way I said it) struck me as extraordinary. The media found it fascinating, and to the Archbishop of York it was a considerable source of worry. He received a steady stream of complaints that the 'unbelieving bishop' of the headlines was clearly unfit to be consecrated. The archbishop was urged to delay my consecration, at least until I made a satisfactory declaration of faith or else was proved to be such a heretic with regard to essential aspects of Christian faith and belief that it would be obvious that I could not become a bishop. The archbishop handled the matter with firmness and calm. When faced with a petition against my consecration, he issued a measured rejection marked by his customary balance between theological erudition and ecclesiastical practicality. I never doubted that I would be consecrated on the date on which he and I had agreed – 7 July 1984.

Although I was rather surprised and somewhat disturbed by the fierce antagonism elicited by my alleged beliefs, I thought that I had stimulated a crucial discussion of Christian faith today that had immense potential for the exploration and enlargement of modern Christianity – an evangelical opportunity beyond the current scope of the church's dialogue with the world. While I much regretted the burden all this fuss placed on the archbishop, otherwise I was not unduly troubled by the adverse press.

As I have explained, I assumed that the target audience of a programme like *Credo* was not the church. I took it for granted that Christian believers knew where their faith was sustained and where it was going. That this assumption proved to be mistaken provided me with one of the major challenges I had to face. My eyes were on the majority of people who have given up belief in the living God and Father of our Lord Jesus Christ (even if they might retain some vague idea about a characterless deity who could be around *in extremis*). It seemed to me obvious that a bishop or any leader of the church appearing on television to expound the faith could not preach the gospel by prosing on about detailed aspects of Christian doctrine or morality. He or she has to engage the viewers' attention about problems they encounter in their own experience in the real world today, hoping that this may catch them up into deeper and broader dimensions of living which extend into God and through him into a more promising future.

Exploring and questions are essential to the dynamic of living faith. It is a pilgrimage, a quest that pulls you on with the hope of being found by more than you know, into possibilities which expand further than you can envisage. So if one is to communicate the good news of the gospel through television and radio, it seems to me that the style used to engage people should be much more like that of a good parish discussion group (where the comfort and intimacy of the group allows the excitement of common exploration) or an engaged tutorial group (where people with a common interest in the area of study build up a shared appreciation of the development of the subject they are studying *together)* – or even of just a set of friends who trust one another to share a journey of exploration and common enlightenment in which all can contribute and from which all may hope to profit. To be lectured by self-styled authorities, reciting what is to be believed about today's world in the language of traditions or documents shaped by the notions of long-dead societies, is boring, unconvincing and irrelevant. There is no lively engagement with our lives and *this* world in which we live.

Religion is a structure that both services and contains our faith. It always has a tendency to become obsolescent and restrictive. The pilgrimage of faith, by contrast, is varied and risky. It is sustained by the rich deposits of previous revelatory encounters experienced by the pilgrims who have gone before; it is maintained by a real (but often fleeting) sense of a Presence and it is always looking *forward* in hope.

When I accepted the producer's invitation to expound my approach to the Christian faith in God, Jesus and the Holy Spirit in today's world I had not yet consciously articulated this understanding myself. So my performance on the *Credo* programme, viewed in isolation, could be seen as verging on a mess and a muddle. But I remain convinced that it was, by the grace of God, appropriate, hopeful and forward-looking. The public clash of both understanding and misunderstanding that followed it raised the right questions – the questions that must be faced if Christian faith is to be heard in today's world as a realistic and promising revelation of the divine dimension that is alive and at work among humanity, for the benefit of our common human future.

So I participated in that recording in good faith, I spoke in good faith and I believe that I opened up the right questions for living by Christian faith and sharing that faith today. I was clear about that then, and I am clear about it now.

4 I discover what is *not* expected of a Bishop

I had no idea as I embarked on my role as Bishop of Durham that I was not behaving in accordance with what was expected as a bishop. A bishop is an authority figure. It took time for me to realize that the general expectation of an episcopal authority figure is that he does not raise questions, engage in discussions or share in the mutual exploration of problems and obscurities – at least not in public. The common assumption is that authority is granted to a bishop only as he confirms the faithful in the various details of belief that they firmly hold to be right.

I would observe that atheists certainly welcome – and expect – such firmness and clarity from bishops. Dogmatism helps to confirm their belief that God is a nonsense. It clarifies precisely what they are rejecting when they dismiss the possibility of the existence of God. I recall years ago hearing a radio discussion between the agnostic Marghanita Laski and the Catholic priest Father Corbishley SJ. She was brought close to impotent rage over what she felt to be the evasive 'Jesuitical' arguments her opponent deployed about what belief in God implied or did not imply. Agnostics find bishops who display signs of agnosticism unsettling and unnatural, especially when such bishops claim that this doubt and search is central to faith.

I am, of course, oversimplifying. I have found my discussions with professed humanists and agnostics, carried on both face to face and through correspondence, one of the most moving strands in my pilgrimage as a bishop. But to return to the impact of my first television appearance before the public as bishop-designate: I must stress how widespread the shock of that impact was to believers, unbelievers and agnostics – not to mention me. What a field day the media had over their 'unbelieving bishop'! Yet I was simply setting out approaches to the Bible and an interpretation of the development of Christian doctrine that had been standard fare in theological faculties for decades and was taught as commonplace in most theological colleges. Furthermore, I was using this approach to explain how it was perfectly possible for a thoughtful modern person today to hold – as I did – to the orthodox belief that Jesus was at the same time both truly God and truly man and to believe (as I most certainly do) in the resurrection of Jesus, whether or not one is convinced by the story of the empty tomb as the account of an indisputable, physical fact.

I probably did not help my case by the relaxed remarks I sometimes let slip. But I could not take the fuss absolutely seriously. I remained clear (perhaps this was overly donnish of me, but I think it was also part of retaining a human perspective) that the only productive approach to realistic and positive discussion of matters of faith or morals is a relaxed approach that is open to questions. I was much amused by a passing comment on me and my foibles made by Conor Cruise O'Brien in *The Observer* during July 1984. Having stated (erroneously) in one article that I did not believe in the resurrection, he gave me credit for being honest but greater discredit for being such a fraud as to go ahead and become a bishop. He concluded: 'I'm the kind of agnostic who likes churches to be *there*. If I need to turn to one one day, I do not want to find it all full of agnostics, in there, looking out at me.'

Just so. Agnostics like to be sure what it is that they are being agnostic about. Therefore Christians must be dogmatic about what they claim – in faith – to know about.

Once Conor Cruise O'Brien had read the transcript of the *Credo* programme, he realized that I did believe in the resurrection. He admitted this and apologized handsomely enough. He suggested why I had been so easily misunderstood. In his second article he wrote, *en passant*: 'Perhaps . . . his complete lack of pomposity and unction contributed to the shock effect.'

I was much encouraged by this recognition of the style of discussion that I was aiming at. Pompous theology, unctuous religiosity – the easy self-righteous assurance that every detail is underwritten by divine authority – can no longer be indulged in. People have to be enticed, led or surprised into thinking things out afresh for themselves.

So there were signs of dawning recognition that I was suffering in a good cause, or at least for a chosen purpose. On the other hand, O'Brien's article drew my attention to the fact that the first word in my interview as broadcast was 'no', while the last word was 'yes'. Both the 'no' and the 'yes', he pointed out, got me into trouble because viewers latched on to them in a way that short-circuited any explanatory exposition that followed.

The explosion of protest triggered by the broadcast highlighted a deep fault-line – if not a fundamental split – within the communities of Christian believers about the very nature and foundations of a living faith in the living God.

On one side of this fault-line stand those who maintain that they adhere to the traditional faith of the long centuries of Christendom – the tradition that encompassed both the Protestant state churches of the sixteenth and seventeenth centuries and the post-Tridentine Catholic Church – a tradition that defines itself by insisting on the unchangeable 'faith that was once delivered to the saints'. These believers are faced across the line by the other group of Christians, those who believe in the pilgrimage faith of modernity (or of 'post-modernity', if that is where we are at present), a way of faith that relies ultimately on exploration and shared experience. This pilgrimage way of faith resonates with many features of the faith on the other side of the fault-line, but it cannot accept the authoritarian and dogmatic definitions by which the traditionalists claim to be entitled to limit discussion of matters of belief and morals.

The split between the two sides is deep, often puzzling, and all too frequently the engine of the most repellent aspects of much Christian talk about God, faith, pilgrimage and discipleship in the modern world. The issue is woven into all the concerns and arguments of this book, so it is as well to spell it out here. I was not so conscious of the clarity of the divide at the time, so in revisiting this period of my life in preparation for this book I was both rather surprised, and fascinated, to find how it leaped out of the records of my first television appearance as a bishop-designate.

At the time, in early summer 1984, I had no idea of the depth and stressful nature of the conflict that I was bringing into the daylight of public discussion. On the whole the publicity intrigued me. It seemed to promise many opportunities for expounding the Christian faith in what I hoped would be an engaging and stimulating way. There was a brisk demand for my presence on radio phone-ins and for radio and television interviews. In my enthusiasm I overdid things at first, as I realized when I briefly lost my temper with a particularly tiresome listener live on air during one late-night phone-in. Mercifully, that particular lapse of concentration was not widely reported. It was, however, a salutary warning to pace myself more carefully. On the whole, though, I enjoyed these encounters: my conversation-partners and I were exploring lively faith today.

So I remained quietly convinced that my contribution to 'Jesus, the Evidence' had been a success. The church at large seemed to be failing to engage with the way most people thought about things these days. Something different – a more exciting approach – had to be tried. I had been given a job – or a call – which offered me the possibility of another ten years of active ministry with unusual access to publicity. If I was to seize the opportunity, it was now or never. I had no plan, only a purpose – the missionary one of sharing more widely with others the God pointed to by the life of Jesus. I assumed that this was the purpose at the very heart of the life and mission of the church. The campaign on which I had launched myself seemed to have set off precisely the open and widespread discussion of what was involved in Christian believing today that was needed. So I thought that I would be recognized by my fellow Christians as being in the mainstream of the faith, worship and mission of the churches. But my opening 'no' and closing 'yes' in that television broadcast confused things.

Philip Whitehead had opened the interview as broadcast by asking whether I held 'that miraculous details of the story of Jesus, like his birth to a virgin or the fact that he walked on water, ought to be taken as representing the literal truth today'. I answered, 'No, but I think it is important to make some distinctions', and went on to detail these distinctions. As it turned out, this seminar style of speaking was courting disaster.

The initial 'no' was either heard to mean (or reported to mean) that I denied that Jesus was anyone special; certainly I was not indicating that he was the man who was God for us and with us. This impression withstood all my positive and orthodox statements on this central point that followed on as the interview progressed, and stuck even despite Whitehead's summing-up at the end of the programme.

Similarly, there was confusion over my answer to Whitehead's last question. He asked me whether someone who says, 'I believe passionately in Jesus as a great moral teacher and a divine agent, and that he is leading me towards God, but I do not believe that he was God-made-flesh,' is still a Christian. Having in mind a number of God-fearers and God-seekers of my personal acquaintance, who pursued their seeking by keeping in touch with the church, my enthusiastic response was 'Yes, yes'. This 'Yes, yes' formed my last words as broadcast in the interview. After the programme they were reported as amply confirming that I denied that Jesus was in any sense divine. My previous positive explanation of how I personally held Jesus to be God with us went unheard and unreported.

The consequent public outcry led the chaplain of the Cathedral Choir School at Hereford, the Revd William Ledwich, to get up a public petition to prevent my consecration. Mr Ledwich cited in support of his petition the 'repeated assertions of Dr Jenkins that he believed neither in the bodily resurrection nor in the virgin birth of our Lord; it was unnecessary, he claimed, for a Christian to believe that Christ was God'. For Mr Ledwich, the implications of my 'no – consider some distinctions' and my 'yes – let us allow an open boundary around the Christian community of faith' in the broadcast were entirely negative. He wanted me out. When, in the end, his efforts to stop my consecration proved in vain, he left the Church of England for the Orthodox Church. His letter of resignation to the Bishop of Hereford claimed that the 14,000 signatures he had gathered on his petition represented only the tip of an iceberg of protest that went unheeded at the church's peril. For Mr Ledwich, the hierarchy's endorsement of me was the last in a long series of betrayals of the Catholic faith by the Church of England and it finally convinced him that the Anglican faith was hopelessly and irredeemably beyond the pale of the One Holy Catholic and Apostolic Church.

Mr Ledwich summed up the burden of his lengthy and detailed letter of resignation in this final paragraph:

> I have made it now clear why I cannot see my way to remaining in the Anglican Church to try to change it. If any human effort was going to change it, the efforts of thousands over the last two months would have done so. The efforts of thousands of thousands since early last century would have stemmed the tide of heresy. The reason why God has not strengthened these efforts is, I believe, because they have been outside the One Holy Catholic and Apostolic Church.

The whole of Mr Ledwich's passionate and tendentious letter reminded me of the notorious statement of Pope Pius IX in his 'Syllabus of Errors', issued in 1864, in which he condemned rationalism, indifferentism, socialism, communism, naturalism, freemasonry, separation of church and state, liberty of the press and liberty of religion, and summed up his ire in the famous or infamous rejection of the notion that 'the Roman Pontiff can and ought to reconcile himself and reach agreement with progress, liberalism and modern civilization'.

The plea to 'stop the world, I want to get off', allegedly made in God's name, seems to characterize religious traditionalists throughout history. Their fearful defensiveness provides a striking argument that religious 'authority', based on revealed faith, is in fact merely an attempt to construct bolt-holes from which to hide from the world as it is. It is an attitude that seems to run directly counter to the claim to believe in a transcendent God who makes himself known to and through men and women of faith in all times.

However, my purpose in writing this book is to explore why I personally continue on in the company of those who go on simply believing in God. At this stage in my story, therefore, I will only register the basic challenge to the possibility of any valid and faithful religious realism that lurked within the response that my television interview provoked among some of 'the faithful' and the consequent arguments they produced against my consecration.

To return to the events as they unfolded. As I have said, in May 1984 I was somewhat surprised by the response from among fellow Christians to the television interview, and perhaps a little bit hurt, but I was not seriously disturbed by it. I did not have the slightest doubt that my consecration would go ahead on its due date.

Now my wife and I were about to go to Hungary for a week's holiday, to visit our daughter Deborah, who was living in Budapest at the time. I needed a new passport and, knowing of my appointment, but unaware of the complications of the sequence of confirmation, which involved designation, election and then consecration,[1] the passport authorities issued my new passport as for 'The Lord Bishop of Durham'. I did not see any objection to this, although I might have received my invitation to visit the embassy in Budapest under slightly false colours. (Although it was just as likely that the invitation was through my daughter, who was by now fluent in Magyar and in regular informal contact with the embassy staff as a British Council student.)

Given the history of doctrinal discussions over the past hundred years, I was bound to be consecrated. The Archbishops of Canterbury and York, along with the majority of the members of the House of Bishops, had received the theological education that I had and, like me, personally stood well within the perspectives of 'liberal

---

1 For an explanation of this procedure, see Chapter 9, p. 94.

orthodoxy'. My writings proved me an impeccable Anglican. My first published book, *A Guide to the Debate about God* (1966), argued for the traditional God who was both transcendent and truly immanent. My second, *The Glory of Man* (1967), was an extended argument for a Christian anthropology (that is, an understanding of what it is, or can be, to be human) that drew on the traditional christology (the doctrine of the person of Christ) of Jesus as God become man, the man whom God chose to become. In 1976, in *The Contradiction of Christianity*, I tackled social and economic issues with particular reference to Marxism, concluding with a chapter on 'The Trinity – Love in the End'. This book met with general approval in the Christian community and was cited, among other places, in lectures by Anglo-Catholic clergy in Eastern Orthodox seminaries. Therefore it was not mere conceit on my part that convinced me that if the fuss over my *Credo* interview escalated somehow to the point where I might be called before some official enquiry, I would have no difficulty whatever in establishing my orthodoxy. So on the morning of 10 May 1984 I took the flight for Budapest with my new passport in my pocket and no worries, looking forward to a happy week.

On my return I resumed my professorial duties, immersing myself in the end-of-year examinations in Leeds and my commitments as an external examiner in St Andrews. The arrangements for my consecration on 6 July in York Minster and the daunting preparations for the move to Auckland Castle, the Bishop of Durham's official residence, had to be fitted in amid all the routine work. Nonetheless, we were determined to keep things as normal as possible. Before the removal van arrived on 10 August, Mollie and I were booked for a two-week Mediterranean cruise with the Swan Hellenic company. A first degree in classics can bring unexpected perks. I had been lecturing on these classical cruises for twenty years and more and was determined that Mollie and I would not have to give up the pleasure merely because I was becoming a bishop.

A researcher ploughing through the newspaper archives for May and June 1984 might well think that I must have been unusually insensitive, or at the very least conceitedly overconfident, in taking the whole controversy so calmly. But I knew my church history. Anglican bust-ups over 'liberal' interpretations of doctrines and the proper interpretation of the Bible have occurred at regular intervals since the 1860s. They occasionally engendered a good deal of heat but they were never settled, and in practice the issues were always left open for further investigation and argument. Progressive Anglicans put this down to the defining Anglican tradition of balancing scripture, tradition and reason as the most appropriate means of guiding faith through developments in human understanding and knowledge. But there had always been vociferous and anxious resistance from the traditional wing of the church, the defenders of 'the faith once delivered to the saints'.

Besides, by the second half of the twentieth century the Church of England had ceased to have the machinery – even if it could muster the will – to enforce an authoritarian crackdown on faith and doctrine. I had grown up in an Anglican tradition that we in the Church of England belonged to one another in order to worship and serve God; our common concern to share the faith implied a duty always to work towards consensus where possible – but that did not mean that we had to agree in every detail of faith and doctrine in order to belong.

As it was, my reliance on my sufficient orthodoxy and the support of the archbishops was justified. My consecration took place on its due date, 6 July 1984. It was what followed after 6 July that began to make plain to me that my missionary-inspired attempts to address matters of faith and doctrine in terms that made sense to contemporary thinking had let some genie out of its bottle. One wing of the church regarded this genie as so divisive and disruptive that if the faith was to be preserved it had to be forced back into its bottle. The other wing of the church, and many seekers outside the church, regarded it as liberating – an opening up of the possibilities of Christian faith to the modern world that was necessary for the universal scope of the Christian gospel.

In addition there was a third school of thought among people who also believed that they held the best interests of Christianity at heart. Their voice was articulated by an editorial in the *Daily Telegraph* of 30 May 1984. According to the writer, my views were

> profoundly destructive of the peace and unity which it is a
> bishop's particular duly to foster . . . what the ordinary man in
> the pew increasingly expects from his bishop is a clear assertion
> of the living Christian tradition he has received. Professor
> Jenkins must now face an unenviable choice. Either to withdraw
> and return to academic life or to press on in the knowledge that
> his election would be pastorally deeply divisive. Many would say
> that, though painful, withdrawal is the wiser choice.

It was this 'quiet life' party which vexed me most. They seemed (to my mind complacently and conceitedly) sure that they knew what the church was for. The purpose of the church was to keep 'the ordinary man in the pew' in the comfort and assurance of the 'peace and unity which it is a bishop's particular duty to foster'. This argument betrays no appreciation of the severity of the challenge that matches the greatness of the promises offered again and again in the Bible. Take, for example, the note sounded in this passage from the letter to the Hebrews.

For the word of God is living and active. Sharper than any double-edged sword, it penetrates even to dividing soul and spirit, joints and marrow: it judges the thoughts and attitudes of the heart. Nothing in all creation is hidden from God's sight. Everything is uncovered and laid bare before the eyes of him to whom we must give account (4.12–13).

It was additionally unsettling that this lofty ignorance of biblical faith was accompanied by the condescending advice that my theology only made me fit for academic life, implying that scholarship has nothing to say to Christian faith. This was a line echoed more than once in letters published in the press – some even written by clergy. The argument was that although it may be perfectly proper for a professor of theology to question and debate in pursuit of the truth of the faith, this is no way for a bishop to behave.

I have always thought that the truth is indivisible and that God is to be served, and known through the mind, whatever level the intellect is operating at. I found the suggestion that I should keep quiet about truths I had discovered through a life of academic study – that I should suppress and modify what I would share with students when I was teaching and preaching to 'the ordinary man and woman in the pew'– frankly blasphemous. If God could not cope with the pursuit of truth, then religion was indeed a sham and the professed concern for those 'in the pew' nothing more than an exploitative fraud.

My experience proved that 'the ordinary men and women in the pew' are quite up to the challenge of using their intellects. Sometimes to my surprise (and delight) the majority responded positively to my teaching and preaching. I still cherish an encounter that proved one of the greatest encouragements I received in my teaching ministry as a bishop. In the second year of my episcopate I went to preach at the church of St Michael and All Angels, Swalwell, an urban parish in Gateshead. Taking its cue from the dedication of the church, my sermon was about angels. I ran through what is known in the theological trade as a process of 'demythologization'. That is to say, I did my best to unpack and express in modern terms what I believe to be at the core of those encounters between human beings and God which were described in biblical times as encounters with an 'angel' or 'angels'. At coffee time afterwards I saw advancing towards me an elderly man whom I had noticed keeping a firm eye on me in the pulpit from his seat in a pew near the front.

I braced myself for what was to come. He stood foursquare before me and informed me: 'I'm not bothered about you now, bishop. I see what you're doing. You're explaining things. You're a *teaching* vicar.'

That was, and remains, one of the great moments in my life. For that was exactly what I believed God had called me to be.

But that day – and many other experiences like it – was yet to come. In May and June 1984 I was rounding off my professorial duties and packing up for the move. I was enjoying the opportunities I was being given by the media to open discussion of the Christian faith, and I was sustained by the knowledge that the majority of my future episcopal colleagues, although they might not entirely approve of my style, shared my 'liberal orthodoxy'. I thought it safe to dismiss the public campaign against me as a temporary fuss that would soon fade away, for my private evidence was that there was an underlying majority of positive interest in what I was trying to achieve.

Between May 1984 and the middle of 1986 I was sent thousands of letters. An incomplete set of 4000 of these were analysed by a professor of sociology at the Open University in the middle of 1986. From the time of the first wave of publicity I received on average between 150 and 250 letters a week from the public. This level of correspondence was sustained for over two years. I am told that was unusual both in number and duration. It is also usual for the majority of unsolicited correspondence arising from publicity to contain protest and complaints. In my case, my mailbag was consistently in my favour. Of the 4000 letters analysed the proportions worked out in the region of five letters in favour of my attempts to open up Christian debate to two against. As far as I know, there was never a day when the encouraging letters were not in the majority. Moreover, up to half the 'anti' letters were of the 'green ink' variety – that is, abusive and incoherent rather than argumentative. This trend was sustained throughout my time as Bishop of Durham. In 1988, when I commented, on a current affairs programme on Easter Day, that the Conservative government's recent budget was 'verging on the wicked' in its impact on welfare provision for the poor, over a thousand letters followed in the next week, of which under a hundred were critical of what I said. This was the most moving – and tragic – mail of all because it included so many sad tales from correspondents from all backgrounds and walks of life, many suffering dreadful poverty, who were desperate for someone to listen to them.

Whatever the views of the vociferous and self-appointed spokespersons reported in the media, I was receiving daily evidence that there were numerous people, both inside and outside the churches, eager to engage with the approach to Christian faith that I was trying to develop.

However, as the weeks passed and the controversy did not die down, I began to read signs that even the bishops who sympathized with me were inclined to take the view that I should pipe down for the sake of peace and quiet. They continued to be friendly to me personally, but I began to suspect that I featured in their minds as something like that description of Cromwell in the historical parody *1066 and All That* – he was 'right but repulsive'. Tactful hints were made that given time these proper issues would be dealt with decently, without all this unpleasant fuss. The church, after all, was for the comfort and assurance of its members, as the *Daily Telegraph* editorial pointed out.

I profoundly disagree with this attitude. The church exists to preach and live by the universal gospel of the salvation and the judgement of God because of the glory and love of God. Authentic and religious comfort – the resources uncovered by faith in God – is derived from our shared worship, service and pilgrimage. Our religious comfort is not the reason for faith. The aim of faith is the service of God. You only have to read the Bible to see that God is at least as much the creative disturber as the purveyor of peace and comfort.

Although I knew this in my heart of hearts, in summer 1984 I simply believed in God and got on with finishing my university work and helping my wife to organize the complicated move to Auckland Castle. (At that time this extremely large house – it was not an actual castle – comprised forty-eight rooms and halls in the domestic part alone; the state rooms included an ancient building that had once been a mediaeval banqueting hall, which at the Restoration was converted into what was said to be the largest private chapel in Europe.)

My wife and I had plenty to occupy us, and I was unaware that within a few weeks the furore prompted by my interview for 'Jesus, the Evidence' – far from dying away – was destined to be outstripped by two further waves of notoriety that would accompany my transformation from professor to bishop.

5 The fault-line becomes an abyss

Events leading up to the consecration proceeded very much as I had expected. The Archbishop of York, Dr John Habgood, met Mr Ledwich and his supporters under the eye of the cameras outside the Archbishop's Palace at Bishopthorpe in York on Sunday 1 July and received their petition to block my consecration. He delivered his reasons for rejecting that petition on Wednesday 4 July. The next day my wife and I made the journey to Bishopthorpe to prepare for the consecration service to be held that Friday.

The archbishop's formal rejection of the petition pointed to the written statement I had given to the clergy of the Diocese of Durham on 22 May to the effect that I would 'respond in good faith and in total dependence on God' to the questions on faith that the archbishop would put to me during the consecration service. Dr Habgood added that, from what he knew of me personally and from his reading of my published works, he had sound reasons to trust in my good faith.

In a comment outside the statement itself, Dr Habgood also added that while the decision to consecrate me was his alone to make, he had consulted with the Archbishop of Canterbury. I knew that I had Archbishop Runcie's support because he had sent me a handwritten note on the day before the decision to go ahead with my consecration was announced: 'We intend to stand by you, and give all possible support to the courageous way in which you have stood so firmly for the truth and I believe your future ministry will justify your claim to be a believing bishop.' With characteristic kindness Bob Runcie added, 'Not only do I welcome you into the House of Bishops but I pray for you as a friend who has often brought fresh air into my own patch of faith.'

Looking back, however, I was struck by one comment that Dr Habgood was reported to have made at his press conference which betrayed that, like the Archbishop of Canterbury and me, he had not yet fully realized just how far my exploratory openness on the 'Jesus, the Evidence' interview had exposed the acute dissonance in the Church of England between the conservative traditionalists on the one hand and the liberal explorers on the other. Dr Habgood commented:

> I want to say loud and clear that he has repeatedly stated that he is a believer in the incarnation and a believer in the resurrection of Christ. What is at issue is not these fundamental Christian doctrines but certain historical claims relating to them.

This was a true statement of my belief. However, the source of the trouble lurked as a subtext under Dr Habgood's last sentence, viz.: 'What is at issue is not these fundamental Christian doctrines but certain historical claims relating to them.' This was perfectly correct from the faith perspective that I shared with both the archbishops and the majority of the House of Bishops. However, for the traditionalists – both of the catholic and the evangelical persuasions – it was essential that these 'historical claims' be defended from any investigation that might lead to their interpretation in the light of modern realities. They had to be guaranteed as being literally true because they were stated in certain biblical texts and were thereby authenticated by divine scriptural warrant as revealed truths. To the traditionalists, therefore, Christian faith depends on the fact that these truths are guaranteed by scripture, endorsed and handed on by the God-granted authorities of the church. If divine authority does not endorse the literal truth of these particular historical claims (such as the virgin birth and the empty tomb) then our faith collapses.

At the time of my consecration I did not recognize that the emerging fault-line between the 'traditionalists' and 'liberals' was in fact such an abyss. I regarded the divisions – as I believe the Archbishop of York and most of my fellow bishops did at the time – as strong differences in emphasis with regard to the presentation of our faith; they were ultimately differences of interpretation rather than disagreement over essentials. We relied on the good faith of all parties, believing that we were all seeking to commend the truth of the Christian gospel and that, whatever our separate perspectives, we knew that gospel to be the one and the same truth.

The reflection afforded me in retirement, along with the challenge of writing this book, has forced me to face the fact that this was a misapprehension. Now I am convinced that the traditionalist view involves an untenable idea of God, one that it is impossible to hold or commend if one takes seriously advances in modern thought since at least the middle of the seventeenth century.

Before I go on with the story of how I was gradually forced to recognize this abyss in consequence of what happened to me from my consecration onwards, I need to recount briefly a couple of stories from the early years of my episcopate which, I believe, illuminate my account of my first turbulent months as a bishop.

I caught my first clear glimpse of the intensity of this divide between the traditionalist and the liberal mindset in relation to

Christian believing in God while taking part in a discussion group that met during a residential meeting of General Synod. The meeting had broken up into small groups to allow time for relaxed conversation about the matters of faith at the centre of the controversy. It was an opportunity to explore one another's views in private, without the aggressive element of public debate. This seemed to me an excellent idea, and for me at least it proved a salutary and revealing experience.

I was rendered speechless by a contribution from a leading evangelical clergyman who was prominent in the campaign rallying conservative evangelicals against the improper laxity of 'liberal' bishops. With great simplicity and obvious sincerity he stated that he would be completely unable to believe in the resurrection of Jesus if he were not absolutely convinced that the Gospel accounts of the incidents surrounding the empty tomb and the encounters with the risen Christ were literally and descriptively true as matters of historical fact. As literal events they 'proved' the resurrection. If they were not literal events, the resurrection was unbelievable.

I was moved by the intensity of his confession, but I was baffled by the tone and content of it. I could not understand how any literate human being of the present day who had compared the narratives concerned could come to the conclusion that they were all literally true and self-sustaining in that literal truth. Perhaps more crucially, I could not see how such a 'literal' truth could 'prove' the resurrection. For me, faith grew out of witnessing to the experiences of a shared faith, which became a shared conviction so vital that it launched a worldwide mission of faith, hope and love. It is impossible to stand outside the faith and point to neutral, literal facts that underpin it.

I had nothing to contribute to the discussion that particular afternoon. I came away with the daunting revelation that the speaker and his fellow believers inhabited a different world from me in a twofold sense. First, their intellectual and emotional approach to assessing what was true was a 'world apart' from mine. Their faith in God, Jesus and the Spirit had the same focus as mine: God as he had revealed himself in Jesus and at work in believers through the Spirit. But their faith was rooted in quite different ground and experience. Secondly, their understanding of the real world in which we all lived had to be a 'world apart' from mine. The speaker's position assumed that his measure of verity – that certain beliefs were guaranteed as literal fact simply because they were recorded in the Bible – would still carry authority under the common assumptions of present ways of thinking today.

In other words, in that discussion group that afternoon I was forcibly struck by the conviction that traditionalists' dependence on mediaeval and even earlier authoritative definitions was bound to trap them in simple credulity, while making the Christian message seem even more incredible to the world at large. In the last decades of the twentieth century certain traditionalist believers were still clinging to interpretations of faith, the Bible and the church that belonged to the middle of the sixteenth century when the popes were determined to resist Copernicus' observation that, contrary to the church's reading of scriptural belief, the earth was not the centre of the universe but a rather small planet in a solar system which proved to be one system among millions.

This resistance to developments in scientific understanding and human knowledge in the name of biblical 'truths' was maintained as the modern world emerged after the Enlightenment. When Erasmus Darwin first sketched out a theory of evolution at the end of the eighteenth century, the journal *The British Critic* complained that he had 'discarded all the authority of the revelation' out of preference for 'the sports of his own imagination'. When his grandson Charles went on to establish his own theory of evolution in *On the*

Origin of Species in 1859, churchmen again dismissed his science as 'contrary to revelation'. As late as 1886, J. W. Burgon, then Dean of Chichester, could write with pompous self-confidence:

> When the Natural Philosopher claims that MAN shall be held to be the product of EVOLUTION – and to be descended from an ape – . . . we are constrained to reject his hypothesis with derision. It is plainly irreconcilable with the fundamental revelations of scripture.

Jump on a hundred years and a bishop-designate is vociferously denounced for claiming in public that a lively and faithful interpretation of the gospel does not necessarily require belief in either a virgin birth or the literal existence of an empty tomb.

One correspondent, signing himself a professor, wrote to the *Church Times* in 1984:

> The New Testament undeniably (I maintain) presents, and means to present, the Virgin Birth and the Empty Tomb as historical events. When will liberals bravely and honestly face this, instead of retreating like cuttlefish emitting a cloud of ink, into obscure, even meaningless, verbiage? Why can't they answer straight: 'This is a false, or at best a pious fraud,' if that is what they believe?

The Gospels were written down by human beings. What the writers of the New Testament meant to present was couched in the terms of their times. As they are no longer available for direct interview, it is only through painstaking scholarship and archaeology that we reconstruct a sense of the cultural language that shapes the way they communicated the wonders and reality of the faith they had discovered and that had found them. Thus the advances of a century of faithful theological scholarship cannot be so summarily dismissed.

Time and again well-educated people, skilled in their professions and disciplines, seem to suppose that their Christian faith can live and operate under entirely different standards of intellect and judgement from those applied in their secular lives. I find it amazing that a 'professor', whatever his discipline, could be simply convinced that biblical texts, narratives and statements of faith can only be treated as if they were as basically literal as elementary formulas in a scientific manual – and if they are not, then the only alternative is necessarily that they are 'pious frauds', deliberately composed to deceive.

The professor's cavalier dismissal – so characteristic of the traditionalist position – of the good faith and serious scholarship of those devout and experienced students of the New Testament who point to other dimensions beyond the merely literal interpretation of biblical texts is no argument at all.

That such positions can still be held is a terrible indictment of the teaching ministry of the churches. The church seems to have failed to communicate to its general membership any realistic awareness of how human understanding of ourselves and the reality that surrounds us must alter our ways of reading and responding in good faith to ancient, sacred and deeply loved and respected texts.

An example of the religious respect still awarded to ignorance that continues to trouble me personally was provided by Lord Hailsham, formerly Quintin Hogg. At Lord Hailsham's memorial service in Westminster Abbey in January 2002, the Dean of Westminster quoted a moving statement of faith by the deceased with which I profoundly agree.

It is knowledge, not error, that presents the real philosophical riddle. It is not evil but good, not darkness but light, not hatred but love, which needs explaining and cannot be explained away. Knowledge, love and beauty and not deviation and failure form both the ultimate mystery and the ultimate reality.

Lord Hailsham was a devout and committed Christian. This made his intervention in the controversy about me all the more personally bewildering and painful. When my views on the resurrection were being hotly debated in the winter of 1984/5, Lord Hailsham wrote a pithy denunciation of me in a letter to *The Times*. His parting shot was that 'I much prefer the word of Matthew, Mark, Luke and John because they were there and David Jenkins wasn't.' He was a devout man, a highly educated man and a lawyer to boot – and yet in his statement of faith he simply dismissed any evidence that did not suit his belief.

Setting aside any findings of critical scholarship over the last hundred and fifty years or so about the authorship of the Gospels, there is no suggestion that either Mark or Luke were contemporaries of the apostles or were present at the time of the resurrection. Even if it were the case (which is not now generally believed) that the Matthew given as the author of a Gospel is the same Matthew listed among the twelve apostles in the Gospels of Matthew, Mark and Luke and in the first chapter of the Acts of the Apostles, nowhere in the Gospels is there any claim that Matthew was a witness to critical resurrection appearances.

The Fourth Gospel features an apostle who might be the apostle John (the son of Zebedee from Galilee) who according to the author of the Gospel – 'John the Evangelist' – accompanied Peter to the empty tomb. The account describes this companion only as 'the other disciple whom Jesus loved' and does not name him. It is quite possible that this 'disciple whom Jesus loved' is meant to be John the apostle, the son of Zebedee, but no direct reference is made to such a named person anywhere in the Fourth Gospel. But even if this uncertain link were valid, the author of the Fourth Gospel (John the Evangelist) could not have been present at any of the resurrection encounters related in the Gospels. It is the judgement of the vast majority of modern scholars that the Fourth Gospel could not have been written by the Galilean fisherman 'the apostle John, the son of Zebedee'. An analysis of the text requires the author to be some later Christian familiar with the cultures of both Judaism and Hellenism around the end of the first century or the beginning of the second century AD – decades after the resurrection of Christ.

These results of careful scholarship may still be unknown territory to the majority of Christian believers. But if history and the knowledge acquired by careful and devout scholarship is pushed aside, how can educated people of today – people trained in the use of their critical faculties – be expected to take 'faith' on the authority of a dogmatic interpretation of a book of 'scripture' governed by quasi-magical rules independent of all criteria used in evaluating other historical texts? Such an approach relegates the 'Holy Bible' to the status of an anachronistic superstition.

This is why I found Lord Hailsham's irritable dismissal so devastating. A simple reading of the Gospels establishes that at least three of the four evangelists named by Lord Hailsham were *not* there. The fact that an otherwise highly intelligent, informed and indeed devout layperson should feel free to pronounce on 'what the Gospels say', without having considered the relevant verses of the New Testament in detail, suggests that responsible or realistic belief is of no importance. What is important is that one's personal beliefs should not be challenged. Christian faith is thus reduced to a matter of spiritual self-indulgence, a shield against disturbing realities so that they don't unsettle one's comfort. Realism, pilgrimage, progress towards the kingdom of God are neither here nor there. The church is the creature of the demands of the faithful; it is there to reinforce what they like to think they know.

As a result of the broadcast of my interview in 'Jesus, the Evidence' I repeatedly encounter similar examples of the comfortable ignorance of self-styled believers, both lay and clerical. The aggressive complaints with which they meet any missionary attempt to reach out into the modern secular reality characterize a neurotic, quarrelling church which at every report makes Christianity ever more unbelievable to the wider world. It was this conflict that increasingly characterized the controversies that took off to greater heights immediately following my consecration.

Despite a certain amount of tension in and around York Minster on the morning of Friday 6 July, my frame of mind remained confident and relaxed. I still assumed that the noise and aggression would soon die away – but I was wrong.

I would gradually learn that – in contrast to my expectation – the majority of Christians did not experience faith as embracing the risk of belief in the community of a pilgrim people whom God is guiding through the wilderness of this world towards the future of his eternal love. For many believers the appeal of faith in God is as a citadel guarded by ecclesiastical dogma resting on assumed scriptural 'facts'. If knowledge of the world challenges ancient interpretations of scriptural data, then that knowledge is to be resisted. Indeed, faith even seems to require resistance to change.

The ministry of openness and exploration to which I had committed myself so enthusiastically plunged me into more controversy and angry confrontation than I had ever dreamed of. From the time of my consecration, events began to teach me hard lessons about the limitations of the present church as a missionary community. I had come to find my own faith through fellowship within the church and participation in the life of the church. So to discover that in their very responses to my ministry fellow Christians were making Christian faith in God less and less credible to our neighbours in the world at large brought me nearer to atheism than I had ever been in my life. In the thick of the controversy at the time I simply persevered in what I thought was the way of faith.

Was this perseverance really about simple belief? Was it perhaps a matter of conceit? The next instalment of my education arose out of a piece of bad luck – or *did* God arrange it so? To consider this I need first to deal with a few matters around the consecration itself.

6 My consecration

A funny thing happened to me on the way to my consecration – or so it seems to me looking back. The evening before the service I attended a session of the York Provincial Consistory Court held within the precincts of York Minister. The ceremony was as ancient as the Minster itself. A dozen mediaeval-sounding documents that served to confirm my right to become Bishop of Durham were read, proved, accepted and signed by a clutch of legal officers. My presence was required in person to declare my consent to election and consecration so that I could be recognized as myself, a safeguard lingering on from mediaeval times against some impostor exploiting local ignorance to slip into the rights, revenues and powers of a Prince Bishop of Durham.

It was all very quaint and highly archaic. I accepted it as a surviving ritual that had to be gone through in order to get on to the consecration service the next morning. When I had taken the required oaths of loyalty to the Queen and of faithfulness to the doctrines of the Church of England, I had to sign the document recording these oaths.

It was the second official document I had signed that evening. Earlier I had signed a document of consent to election. I did so with my normal signature, the one I use on cheques and suchlike. But now the procedures had been satisfied, I had taken the oaths and I was legally Bishop of Durham. So I signed that second document with my episcopal signature, 'David Dunelm:'.[1] As I signed, it occurred to me that it was rather like the old-fashioned procedure of a just-married wife signing the marriage register with her husband's name. Of course in my case the change in personal identification was not permanent. The signature lasts only for the duration of the diocesan post. Without any conscious premeditation I signed that document keeping the usual florid capital 'D' for my Christian name that I had used since a boy. For the 'D' of Dunelm:, however, I used a stark capital without any flourishes.

I stuck to these differentiated capitals throughout my time in office. I did not plan to do so; indeed it was some time before I noticed the distinction myself. But I think it was a subconscious response to the pressure of what was happening to my public persona in the media. The media reputation – the public face assigned to me – was a caricature only ambiguously connected with David Edward, the baptized Christian disciple who was still trying to pursue his discipleship, however ineptly or outrageously. The distinction between the two – the public caricature and the personal pilgrim – became important for me in keeping my balance through certain more depressive moods.

As far as I understand it, Christianity is the most *personal* of religions. As I had tried to communicate in the *Credo* interview, the good news is that God himself, personally, has become one of us. I was clear that God's call to me to do this job involved my doing it in a way that meant my being me *more*, not less. God had taken the risk of calling me. I (with the magnificent and moving support of

---

1 A diocesan bishop in the Church of England acquires a new signature as a 'Lord Bishop'. In the case of the Diocese of Durham the bishop joins his Christian name to 'Dunelm:'. The colon represents a shortened form of a late Latin adjective 'Dunelmenis', that is, 'of Durham'.

my wife) had taken the risk of responding. I could trust God to see me through, one way or another. By this I do not mean that God would guarantee that what I did would be right, but rather that I could 'sin boldly' and still hope for God's correction and sufficient resources to enable me to persist in the task I was appointed to, namely, to help people to recognize the proffered invitation to participate in the sharing and love of God.

On the eve of my consecration I had not yet come to terms with the personal impact of becoming a senior bishop in the established Church of England. The vital and troubling point for me then (which still remains so to some extent now) was that the abrupt change in my public image was, in one sense, nothing to do with *me*. I – David Edward Jenkins – had not changed in my faith, discipleship, or the preaching and teaching that I had developed during my forty years of ministry. I had to come to terms with the 'accidental' fact (or might it have been a call from God?) that I was personally obscured and hindered by a straw man – 'the Bishop of Durham' – who was not seen as a human being and fellow pilgrim but as a figurehead who was expected to accommodate all sorts of expectations, fantasies and neuroses lurking among both the faithful and the public at large about what 'Christianity really meant'.

For me faith is a journey of discovery into the reality and possibilities of God. It is a pilgrimage pursued in the company of other seekers, first those within the mainstream of the Christian tradition, but also with all those committed to the pursuit of humane concerns from other faith perspectives. I personally had come to my conviction of faith in and through the Anglican community. It was natural, therefore, that I should pursue my calling through the Church of England as effectively as I could. But my pilgrimage had led me to the conviction that faith in God could not be trapped within the dogmatic demands of any particular Christian community or tradition. Dogmas are always orientated on the past. The God whom I had glimpsed was to be encountered in the present and his relationship with us was orientated on the future. Everything we 'know' is therefore provisional, held together and given direction by faith, the faith that trusts and hopes in the love of God and the resources of the Holy Spirit.

I had not consciously formulated this personal perspective with such clarity when I took the plunge into the opportunities I saw opening up before me as I became a more public figure. Hence I was entirely taken by surprise by the furore that met my first television interview as bishop-designate. I was increasingly shocked and troubled by the fierceness of the opposition that steadily built up against me from within the church. I found its uncompromising and dismissive nature the most difficult aspect to come to terms with. For despite the fact that I disagreed with many of my opponents' interpretations and emphases, I continued to believe that the faith of those who were so vociferous against me was rooted in, and directed towards, the same God as my faith, and that we shared the same basic convictions about the relationship of Jesus to God. And yet, while I assumed that they and I existed within the same 'household of faith', they were certain that I was *outside it.*

This baffled me and sometimes depressed me. I could not understand it at the time. I see now that the issue was the dynamic and logical link between living in faith and enjoying certainty. This, in fact, is what this book is about. I began it to explain how I simply believe in God. It became an exploration of how I can continue to simply believe in God. It is my account of living in faith; how I came in faith, what faith led me into and where I believe it is leading now.

As soon as I became a bishop and – as I thought – acted accordingly, I was repudiated by many of those whom I thought of as fellow faithful believers on the basis of what appeared to me to be secondary issues related to our shared Christian faith in God. It has taken me a long time to realize that the fulcrum of this often bitter controversy was the issue of *certainty*.

The matter of certainty is crucial, for it lies at the heart of the *credibility* of any Christian (or, indeed, any theistic) faith in God in the modern world as it has emerged in the last three hundred years or more. To put it briefly now for further discussion later: there can be no certainties about faith (save faith itself) – only assurance, commitment and exploration in hope and worship.

Before I return to my narrative of the events through which I became conscious of this understanding of faith in God, I need to register another point.

Because I was convinced of the impossibility of certainty in connection with reasons for faith, I became certain that those Christians who claimed certainties were wrong. But this does not mean that I believe that such people are excluded from being – in some real and hopeful way – fellow pilgrims on the way of faith towards the same true God. By God's grace, we are not excluded from his love by making mistakes about him; even mistaken, we may still make genuine attempts to serve him and know him better.

So I would argue that my certainty differs from the certainties of my critics in that being so clear that uncertainty is inevitable, I am free to collaborate with any Christian believer who is willing to collaborate with me. In contrast, those Christians who demand certainties as essential to belief must be exclusive. In the end, demanding certainty about faith is essentially schismatic (as is illustrated by the wretched history of Christian quarrelling). The central question for the future of Christian faith is whether it is possible to attain sufficient assurances of faith to sustain realistic hope while at the same time deepening humility and opening us up to deeper truth.

I had barely sensed these questions, let alone formulated them, by the time I arrived at York Minster on the feast of St Thomas More, that Friday 6 July, for my consecration service. My mood as I walked in the procession up the nave was businesslike and, I hope, quietly prayerful as I simply believed that I was following my call to serve God.

Whatever my own personal mood, the atmosphere around the Minster was fairly tense. There was a large crowd of journalists outside the west end, interspersed with a few protesters carrying placards. The stewards posted at the doors were briefed to admit only ticket-holders to the service.

The service was in fact interrupted twice. As Professor Nineham, the preacher, was shown into the pulpit to give his sermon a man stood up in the nave, gesticulating and shouting: 'You want to stop this. Let no more denigration be brought on Jesus Christ. This is invalid.' Two vergers accosted him and he apparently said, 'I have said my piece – I'll go,' and was escorted out.

Later in the service, when I had been presented to the archbishop, and the chief legal officer (the Vicar General) of the Province of York was preparing to read out the royal mandate for my consecration as Bishop of Durham, a clergyman walked out from the body of the congregation to plant himself before the lectern. Interrupting the Vicar General he began to shout and protest against me. As his voice faded down the church various shouts of counter-protest were heard from the congregation. (One of our family guests at the service, a professor's wife, who was rather a conventional lady, confessed to my wife afterwards that she had surprised and embarrassed herself by being so moved by her sense of outrage as to shout out loud in church.) The protester was later identified as an evangelical clergy-man, Mr Mowll. Outside, interviewed by the *Guardian*, Mr Mowll admitted that 'he had never met the new bishop, nor had he heard the television programme, or seen a script of what he was supposed to have said. He had just read about it in the newspaper.' Apparently, before the service he had leafleted the members of the congregation as they entered, calling on them to follow his exit 'as a protest in favour of the truth'.

No one followed Mr Mowll out. The archbishop suggested we had a moment of silence and then continued with the service. Holy communion passed off peacefully and properly. Although certain members of my family party had been distressed to the point of tears, the rest of the service went smoothly.

In the sunshine outside afterwards the archbishop and I responded briefly to some friendly questions from the assembled press. A reporter from the *Church Times* recorded his impressions:

> Professor Jenkins, now Bishop Jenkins, and still obviously affected by the warmth and length of the applause at the end of the service which rang out through the Minster for nearly two minutes, said: 'It was a splendid service. When people care about things you do get into arguments, but you must carry on and look ahead. It has been a simply splendid day.'

The only answer I remember giving was in response to someone who asked me what I was going to do now. With incautious jollity I replied: 'Go home, lie low and say nuffin.' This journalist failed to pick up the reference to Brer Rabbit, and at least one paper reported that I had indicated my intention – now that I was a properly consecrated bishop – to moderate my controversial views. I had merely meant that I intended to go home and have a quiet weekend off.

7 'Ye have not passed this way heretofore'

When a bishop is consecrated, he has the privilege of choosing the preacher for his consecration service. I invited an old friend to give the sermon at mine. I first met Professor Dennis Nineham at The Queen's College, Oxford, when I was an undergraduate there after the war. Between 1947 and 1952 I took degrees first in classics and then in theology, and Dennis was one of my theology tutors. He had a distinguished career, holding professorships at London University and Cambridge – where he was Regius Professor for a time – moving on to become Warden of Keble College, Oxford. In 1984 he was Professor of Theology at Bristol University.

Within theological circles Dennis Nineham was regarded as a fairly 'radical' liberal, and my invitation to him to preach at my consecration was regarded by some of my critics as a deliberate provocation. In fact, when I issued my invitation I was not aware that there was a war looming about the nature and future of Christian faith. I thought that I was making a creative contribution to the discussion that was necessary if Christianity was to be opened up as an exciting and saving possibility to the average denizen of the modern world. Dennis seemed just the man to address the task of reinvigorating the faith for today. And although I had not briefed him in any way, his sermon turned out to be magnificently appropriate.

Reading the sermon now, at this distance, I find it even more apt than I recognized at the time. It was long and substantial, and I do not suppose that many of the two thousand people in York Minster that morning would have absorbed a great deal of it.[1] One epigrammatic sentence near the end struck me very forcibly: 'Bishops, it has been said, are – generally speaking – generally speaking.' I took this to heart and vowed that whenever I made public pronouncements I would always strive to come down to earth with some specific and relevant examples and relevant applications. It was an approach that would get me into further trouble – witness my enthronement sermon (of which more later). With every example I knew I was taking a risk and I would never claim the status of a 'word from God' for anything I said. My intention was only to illustrate the earthly applications of what I was saying about God and how this sort of question might suggest that people who cared for the common good ought to respond with this type of action.

Although this approach contributed to my notoriety, I have always been grateful to my old tutor for giving me this challenge. All too many sermons, to my mind, are tainted by what the schoolboy is supposed to have said about biblical parables, that they were 'heavenly stories with no earthly meaning'.

In his sermon Dennis Nineham addressed an issue that I consider absolutely central to an understanding of Christian faith and Christian theology in our world today. He took his text from the Old Testament book of Joshua, 3.4: 'Ye have not passed this way heretofore.' This comes from the account of how Joshua took over as leader of Israel and mediator between God and his people after the death of Moses. Moses had delivered the chosen people from slavery

---

1 The full text is published in *Theology*, LXXXVII, September 1984, pp. 361–70.

in Egypt. Moses was dead. Who would lead the chosen people into the Promised Land? Joshua.

Joshua ordered the people, led by the priests and the ark of the covenant, to cross the river Jordan in the direction of Jericho and thus enter the Promised Land. Thus this was an epoch-making move. Joshua chapter 3 relates how Joshua told the people to keep well behind the priests so that they could see exactly where they were going under the guidance of God, and follow on. They needed such guidance because 'ye have not passed this way heretofore'. The Bible is telling us the story of how the people whom God chose for his prophetic and revelatory relationship made a new and decisive move into entirely unknown territory. God's people have to move on.

This dynamic of being on the move towards the fulfilment of God's purposes is absolutely central to biblical faith.

With the aid and inspiration of the Holy Spirit, the apostle Paul and other followers of Jesus came to the conclusion that in his resurrection of Jesus from the dead God had made it clear that the 'Chosen People' were not confined to one race or one land. 'There is neither Jew nor Greek, there is neither bond nor free, there is neither male nor female; for ye are all one in Christ Jesus' (Galatians 3.28). This is a clear affirmation of the potentially absolute universality of the concern and purpose of God. The true and living God is God of all for all. The Christian churches have never lived up to this call to universality. Indeed they have regularly ignored it, forgotten it and betrayed it. And yet universality remains at the very heart and dynamic of that Christian faith that the New Testament strives to express.

I put Professor Nineham's chosen text in its broader perspective here in order to highlight a dynamic strand in my understanding and practice of Christian faith and discipleship – the part the use and power of the Bible plays in my continuing simply to believe in God. To put it briefly now, I grow ever more convinced that reflective and systematic study of the biblical texts opens one's mind, heart and soul to interlocking and ever-expanding insights into the purposes of God. I regularly meet the presence of God in my own meditations on the Bible. I hasten to add that I do not believe that God tells me things directly. Rather, I am opened up to seeing something more clearly, find my hope restocked, my perseverance recalibrated more closely to the purposes and the presence of God. Similarly, in opening my sermons as I do – 'In the name of the Father, and of the Son, and of the Holy Ghost' – I am repeating in hope a constant prayer that the Spirit of God will bring something revelatory out of my words, both for my hearers and for myself. I am not claiming God's authority for what I say. I am offering what I have to say in the hope that God will stir some response within those who hear me which will be a blessing and move us on in faith.

To return to Professor Nineham's sermon: the text 'ye have not passed this way heretofore' led him into his theme that the immense changes in thought and culture that have transformed the West over the last two hundred years or more mean that Christianity now exists in a very different spiritual and practical climate from that of its first sixteen or seventeen hundred years. For today's Christians it is literally true that as far as practising and commending Christian faith in God is concerned, we 'have not passed this way heretofore'.

Professor Nineham pointed out that the traditional dogmas and creeds of the Christian church were worked out – through a great deal of fierce controversy – in the years of the late Roman empire. The creeds we still use today, the central picture or doctrine of God as Holy Trinity, the belief in Jesus as a real man who was 'in person' God among us, were all hammered out in the fourth and fifth centuries AD. As doctrinal formulations they were fixed in their present definitions as the Roman empire was invaded from north and central Europe, Barbarians captured Rome and the empire in the West collapsed.

This may seem a remote and irrelevant history lesson, but in fact it is absolutely crucial to a realistic understanding of the dilemmas Christians find themselves facing today about the nature of Christian belief.

In his consecration sermon, Professor Nineham explained the historical context so clearly that I think the following paragraphs are worth quoting at length:

> Hardly had the bishops dealt with the need for adjustment
> and restatement when the Roman empire fell, to be succeeded
> by a civilization, if civilization it can be called, markedly
> inferior to it. This is important, and two things need to be
> said about it. First: because this period was so aware of its
> cultural inferiority, it was essentially backward-looking.
> Believing that their predecessors had known more about every
> subject than they would ever know, the people of this time
> came near to absolutizing the past and thinking that the truth
> had already been discovered and declared in days gone by.
> They simply looked back to what they took to be more or less
> infallible authorities – men such as Hippocrates and Galen,
> for example, in medicine; Pythagoras and Euclid in math-
> ematics; Plato and Aristotle in philosophy; Isaiah, Jesus,
> Paul, Athanasius in religion.
>
> The second thing to emphasize about this period is how
> long it lasted. For some one thousand or twelve hundred
> years European culture remained remarkably static. Even at
> the end of this period the countries of Europe were still non-
> industrial, non-mechanized societies with methods of

agriculture, means of communication and an outlook on natural science not radically different from those of their predecessors; and their horizons, so far as concerned matters of astronomy, cosmology, chronology, psychology, medicine and all the rest, were not much wider than those of the early Christian period.

In a situation like that it was possible with complete integrity to believe more or less exactly what had been believed for centuries and to express it without reservation in the age-old words and symbols. And that is what people in fact did; they did it for ten or twelve centuries. And when a thing has been going on as long as that it comes to seem unchangeable, just part of the way things are. So it came to seem that the essence of being a Christian – or at any rate an essential part of it – was to be able and willing to believe exactly what had been believed in the past and to express it without remainder or reservation in the traditional terms . . .

Long though this period lasted, it was only one particular period of the church's history . . . and it is now over. There has been a gigantic cultural revolution in the last two hundred years or so. Change has taken place on a scale, and at a speed, quite unprecedented in modern human history, and it has produced what we call 'the modern world' or 'the modern West'. Civilization is widely – I had almost said 'wildly' – different from the one I have been describing, or any that have gone before . . . Verily, 'ye have not passed this way heretofore'. Do not be misled by the truth that God does not change. Many things do not change; for example, illnesses such as tuberculosis or diabetes, but our ways of understanding and relating to them change a great deal – after all, you would not have much faith in a doctor who treated your complaint by applying leeches to suck your blood, which was the up-to-date treatment in the sixteenth century. Why should it be any different with the theologian?

'Why *should* it be any different with the theologian?' Indeed, why should it be any different with any thoughtful Christian who has an awareness of a call from God to follow his purposes in the modern world?

The Bible introduces the true and living God in its very first chapter with the splendidly hopeful affirmation: 'And God saw everything that he had made and, behold, it was very good' (Genesis 1.31). Such a God cannot be defined for all time in formulations forged under particular circumstances of history and culture. We will always need to test our knowledge as we seek God in our times and we must allow ourselves to be shaped by him on the way to his future. This would seem to me to be the essence and dynamic of any theistic belief in a God of revelation who is known through the Holy Spirit.

History has not stopped. Human development has not stopped. Has God stopped? An atheist would give the short answer that God has not stopped because he never started – 'God' is nothing but a human invention. My faith denies this short answer, but I cannot ignore those of my fellow believers who appear to want to keep God to themselves rather than hope that God will open us out and enlarge us to include all in the possibilities of his ultimate creation.

The theistic religions need to answer the question, where does a transcendent God stop? Does God stop in a nation state established in the Promised Land as defined by the Torah? Does God stop in a Qur'anic *ummah* ruled by *shariah* law? The question becomes focused on the issue of 'scripture' – those collections of written texts sacred to the theistic traditions: the Torah, the Bible and the Qur'an. If these scriptures represent the 'last word' on what the faithful must believe about God and the world, do they prevent attempts to develop any new creative and future-looking developments in the pilgrimage to which we believe God to be calling us? If so, then the theistic religions of revelation are in head-on collision with the scientifically aligned and experimentally shaped world of today.

If that is the choice – between religion and realism – then I must go with the humanists. I cannot believe in a God who has no connection with the amazing human capacity for discovery, invention and creativity that has burgeoned with such results (even if some of them are threatening and ambiguous) over the last three hundred years or more. I would be in danger of associating myself with religious bigotries and sectarianism if I was not convinced that the vast majority of believers were somehow in at least intermittent touch with the living God who himself takes the risk of our sins for the sake of our growth, in freedom and grace, so that we may work with him towards the fulfilment of the amazing potential of our humanity.

This is the absolute crux of faith, hope and of love for me. If religious faith must be tied to authoritarian rejections of human development since the sixteenth or seventeenth centuries, then it is hopelessly outmoded bigotry – superstition constructed to shelter our religious fantasies of hope and sustain the material power of our religious organizations.

I do not believe that this is what Christian faith is about. The Bible teaches us that human beings are 'in the image of God', which implies that our horizons are practically limitless, and yet most of the time religious organizations fail to live up to the divine potential in the human spirit. I shall return to this later, but for now I insert this explanation here because I see now just how basic an issue

I was raising in my attempts to act appropriately as a bishop and how precisely my old tutor and friend focused on that issue in his sermon.

My re-reading of the sparse file of newspaper clippings I have kept from that July underlines this impression. It includes an article from *The Times* written by Clifford Longley (then their religious affairs correspondent) published on 9 July, the Monday following my consecration. Under the headline 'Churchmen air their doubt about liberal theology', Longley dismisses the theological perspective shared by Professor Nineham and myself.

> The standard defence of radical reinterpretations of Christian doctrine is that the modern, secular, sceptical mind cannot be expected to apprehend Christian truth unless it is translated into terms more in harmony with the spirit of the age. This was the message of Professor Dennis Nineham, Professor of Theology at Bristol University, in his consecration sermon in York on Friday.

This is a misunderstanding, or possibly a deliberate misinterpretation. Professor Nineham's argument was not about translating Christian truth into terms that were in harmony with the spirit of the age; it was that the expansion of human knowledge since the late seventeenth century has drastically altered our understanding of the very processes of the world. In the light of evolution and science things look very different to us from the world-view that dominated the first twelve hundred years of Christianity. The believers who formulated the Christian doctrines in the fourth and fifth centuries had no concept of process, let alone progress. Now we understand everything in a radically different context.

Longley goes on to argue that:

In fact, as the popularity of cults, astrology, reincarnation and general irrationality demonstrates, the spirit of the age is as credulous as ever it was. A virgin birth two thousand years ago is nothing compared with what many decent, intelligent, educated folk are willing to believe.

This is true, but irrelevant to the main issue. There are always people ready to believe anything – or almost everything. Every age is full of credulity. The question responsible human beings must wrestle with in every age is that of *credibility*. What is a proper criterion of credibility in our own time and our present world? Can we reach a responsible and mutual assessment of truth and realism today without taking full account of modern methods of thought, based on scientific and experimental standards – methods that have been established by their results over the last three hundred years? As I have said – can it really be that God has stopped, having deposited the saving truth of his gospel in the hands of ecclesiastics peering back into a world the rest of humanity left behind centuries ago?

In Longley's view:

It is a characteristic of the modern liberal school to want to knock away authority, whether of scripture, of the creeds or of the church, and so replace it by private mental experiences as the ultimate test.

This is not true of the 'liberalism' that I am committed to. The community of faith is essential to the existence and sustenance of my own faith. What I am trying to establish is what sort of authority – 'whether of scripture, of the creeds or of the church' – is realistically available to us today. The issue is that of the limitations of authority and whether it is locked in past formulations.

The real and insidious sting of Longley's argument comes in the tail of his article:

> . . . Only an Herculean intellectual effort can bring even a glimpse of what is at stake. It needs a profound critique, first of all, of the whole Western intellectual climate since Descartes and the Enlightenment, and what it says may be of fundamental relevance not just to a few relatively obscure academics.

His reasoning echoes Pope Pius IX's 1864 rejection of the notion that the Roman Pontiff should in any way reconcile himself to 'progress, liberalism and modern civilization'. In 1870 Pope Pius IX called a general council to reinforce his position by passing a decree of papal infallibility. The council barely managed to complete its business before Garibaldi and his army arrived to liberate Rome on their mission to unite Italy and create the modern nation state. Thus, standing Canute-like before the tide of modernity, the pope registered the claim of the Christian traditionalists today: human history may render us irrelevant but we hold the guarantees of eternity.

This denial of the possibility of any revelation from God in modern history is echoed in Longley's closing reference to the need for 'a profound critique . . . of the whole Western intellectual climate since Descartes'.

The French philosopher Descartes died in 1650, a year after the Peace Settlement of Westphalia brought an end to the Thirty Years War. In that war the Catholic and Protestant monarchs of Europe fought themselves to a standstill trying to establish their competing versions of the 'true religion' that should be imposed on all people and govern all Christian behaviour. Religious tolerance grew from a stalemate. It had become obvious to the ruling powers of Europe that attempts to enforce religious agreement in faith and morality was neither feasible nor worth the terrible human cost.

Witnessing the costs of those prolonged religious power struggles, Descartes felt compelled to seek out an alternative source of certainty and truth independent of 'the church'. He came up with the famous formulation *Cogito ergo sum* (I think, therefore I am), from which intellectual starting-point followed the developments of the Enlightenment and modern philosophy.

It is not possible to reach back behind these 'secular' developments to some pure deposit of mediaeval or early Christian truth that is valid as such and in its traditional formulation for all succeeding history. Human beings – whether believers in God or not – are part of the irreversible historical process. It is right for believers in God to seek help from the past to discern God in the present, but they have to keep their focus on his future. The claim that the stamp of revelation authorizes one to ignore either history or science only guarantees that any form of belief in God will appear to the wider world to be an outmoded superstition.

Therefore the matter Professor Nineham addressed in the sermon he preached at my consecration is absolutely central to the responsible exposition and hopeful practice of faith in God today. To want to 'stop the world', to hide from the material world, is essentially faithless. We are not called to be faithful ostriches burying our heads in the deposits of the religious past. The sacred formulations of past believers are rich resources to be read in the light of our present reality – both historical and scientific – as we present believers strive to live and expound faith in God today.

8 The lightning: my notoriety goes worldwide

My consecration was over and I left York that Friday afternoon for a quiet family weekend back in Leeds. During the night of the following Sunday, 8 July, at around 2 a.m., the roof of the south transept of York Minster burst into flames. Through the night firemen battled to contain the ferocious blaze as it spread through the ancient wood beams. By morning grave damage had been done, but the fire had been put out within the south transept.

During the exhaustive investigations that followed, by the fire brigade, the insurance companies and the Minster authorities, no firm conclusion was reached as to the cause of the fire. One theory was that a chemical treatment recently applied to the roof beams had reacted with another substance in the heat of that summer night and ignited debris lying about between the rafters; others suspected arson (an arsonist had been at work among churches in the York and Durham dioceses in the previous few months). However, the media and certain members of the public had an alternative theory. The fire was caused by a bolt of lightning. This was a classic 'act of God' – a gift both to those who had decided that I was not fit to become a bishop and to a delighted media.

Early on the morning of Monday 9 July I left home, oblivious of the events in York, to catch a train to Birmingham where I was due to attend a meeting as President of the Institute of Religion and Medicine. When I arrived at my destination I was met with news of the fire and a message from my daughter Rebecca to call home urgently. I did so, to discover that journalists had been ringing up for my comments. My daughter, who had taken the calls, told me that when the first journalist suggested to her that the fire was the result of a divine bolt of lightning, her immediate response was light-hearted: 'But surely people don't still believe in the god Thor? Besides, God can't be that inefficient – he missed my father by a good two days.' Neither she nor I could take this outbreak of super-stition seriously.

As I look back now to the events of the week after my consecra-tion I am surprised to find how indifferent I was to being labelled the fraudulent bishop whose lack of belief caused God to set York Minster on fire. I was very sorry to hear that part of so magnificent and sacred a building had been so badly damaged – but it had nothing in particular to do with me. So when Rebecca informed me of the developing media story that the fire was believed by some to be caused by a jealous God expressing his displeasure with me by means of a thunderbolt, all I can remember thinking is: Fancy that! Whatever next?! I went back to my meeting in Birmingham and scarcely gave the matter another thought. As far as I was concerned, my consecration service had passed off with only minor disturb-ances, a magnificent sermon and a heart-warming expression of support from the congregation. I was ready to get on with my ministry and engage in whatever tasks and opportunities presented themselves to me.

However, as that week wore on, signs pointed to the depths of the disturbance I had stirred up. Far from dying away, the 'lightning story' gathered pace. By 11 July the Archbishop of York felt impelled to write to *The Times* from an important meeting of the World

Council of Churches in Geneva to which he had gone, reluctantly leaving York early that Monday morning after receiving the news that the fire was out. After expressing his gratitude for all the sympathy and help offered in response to the Minster fire, Dr Habgood wrote:

> I feel I must point out the disturbing implication of those letters which somehow seek to link the fire with some remarks made by a bishop-elect on a TV discussion programme. What kind of a God do your correspondents believe in? I grant that if we still lived in biblical times, and if it was customary to treat thunderstorms as some kind of messengers from God, then the connection might seem inevitable. But have we learned nothing in the intervening years about how God works in his world? . . . To interpret the effect of a thunderstorm as a direct divine punishment pushes us straight back into the kind of world from which the Christian gospel has rescued us.
>
> Is illness a divine punishment? Ought we to ask after a car crash whether the car was carrying some outstanding sinner? I hope your correspondents have thought through the implication of their hasty judgements. If their answer is that they have, then perhaps all that needs to be said is that this difference between the *two* theologies [my emphasis] is precisely what the 'Jenkins affair' is all about.

Temperamentally and politically Dr Habgood was not always in sympathy with the ways in which I insisted, throughout my episcopate, on pressing what I saw to be the practical and evangelical importance of identifying the gulf between the two theologies, but any disagreement between us was over tactics, not substance. Even though, as an archbishop responsible for the running of the Church of England, he must often have found my importunate question-raising a trial, privately Dr Habgood was always very supportive of me and never publicly gave way to the exasperation that I am sure he felt at times over my regular appearances in the headlines.

Despite Dr Habgood's intervention, the 'lightning strike' theory spread right around the globe. I was sent news reports from papers across the United States, Australia, New Zealand, South Africa, India, Japan and the Middle East, not to mention most Western European countries. God and the Bishop of Durham became a worldwide topic which for a while at home in the UK featured almost daily in press and radio and on television.

It began to dawn on me just what I had launched myself into. What was all this notoriety about and how was I to respond to it? I was in my sixtieth year when I became a bishop, and in view of what I had learned during my long pilgrimage of faith in God, it would never occur to me to take seriously the proposition that God might send a bolt of lightning as a direct intervention to express his displeasure at my theology. And yet I was facing a substantial (or at least certainly vocal) constituency of concerned Christians who claimed that the lightning could have come from God – for, they argued, the Bible is full of such signs and interventions. The divide between us was no mere difference of emphasis in details of the Christian faith. The lightning had revealed, as the archbishop's letter to *The Times* implied, two very different theologies based on deeply different understandings of the nature and being of God.

Given that we were, therefore, in contest over fundamentals about how God relates to the material universe and the human persons within it, the fierceness of the debate was perhaps not to be wondered at – but it did get fierce.

Whatever the sincerity of my opponents, I could not help wondering about the note of fear that sounded through their response to me. What concerned me most amid all the self-righteous anger was the spectacle we were making of Christianity to the outside world. The very fact that Christians were entering into sincere public debate over the question of whether a true God flung lightning bolts about could only prove to the rest of the world that we were a foolish bunch of fantasists.

So few believers – within all the faith communities – seem to be aware that the central issue for anyone who claims faith in a transcendent and loving God today is whether such a God could possibly exist at all. Typically, the vocal and self-proclaimed defenders of the 'Truths of Faith' maintain that the world must be seen in terms of their faith-understanding: what they and their group of believers customarily declare to be the truth of our church and our scriptures is indeed 'The Truth' and so definitive of reality. In other words, in order to be faithful to God and his revelation, true believers are expected to ignore the workings of what is, by faith, supposed to be God's world. It is the fierceness and firmness of conviction that counts. God has nothing to say to us or show us through our understanding of the world.

I have to confess that it is only now that I am facing up to just how angry I am about this. There is a disturbing issue here about the ungodly behaviour of the faithful. The most uncomfortable impression that sticks in my mind from those days of controversy is how little Christian spokesmen and women displayed concern for either truth or the engagement of the gospel. I was very disappointed with the way in which my critics concentrated on criticizing my views as – on very inadequate evidence – they believed them to be. Whatever my motives, I had succeeded in getting a discussion of God, Jesus and the faith on to the media. And yet my vociferous critics did not grasp the opportunity to engage the attention of the indifferent and the curious with their personal positive and exciting versions of the Christian faith as it captivated them, enriched their lives and illuminated reality. I could understand that they might be saddened by my account of faith, but then why did they not cheer-fully counter with their own understanding – hoping that God could use us all? The majority of my critics gave the appearance of not so much being concerned with preaching the gospel to the world as with defending themselves within the fortress of their own faith.

I was also sincerely shocked by the argument circulated by several respectable and even learned critics that it was quite in order for me to hold – and even to express – my views as a scholar and a profes-sor, but that the same views were inappropriate from the mouth of a bishop. I found this appalling. Now that I had become a bishop I was expected to lie for the sake of the faithful – or at the very least conceal truth-seeking questions from them. Such an argument speaks volumes about the mind-numbing condescension with which many clerical and church authorities continue to regard the laity. It echoes Dostoevsky's Grand Inquisitor: to avoid trouble, to keep people docile and happy, you must avoid the sort of risks Jesus took. Religions are about order and comfort. They are nothing to do with the blazing creativity, the searching glory and the wondrous risk of God's love.

So although I dismissed the lightning strike story at the time, I now see how diagnostically significant it was. Until the Minster fire I had taken it for granted that modern, thoughtful believers in God could never entertain the idea that the living God of the Bible might arrange lightning strikes to convey personalized messages in the twentieth century. That fire brought me into public confrontation with a vociferous crowd of Christian believers who were quite sure that God had sent lightning as an explicit sign of his disapproval of my faithless dismissal of key parts of his revelation as set out in the Bible. The meat of the matter appeared to be a straightforward confrontation between believers who followed a God of signs and certainties and pilgrim believers and explorers who followed a God of creative risk and reality.

In fact this debate was highly privatized. It ignored the wider context of the society in which it was taking place, a society in which the climate of opinion assumed that there was no God. This wider arena of the contemporary world was precisely where I believed God had called me. The God who had found me was not primarily to be engaged within his church. He had chosen to risk working out the purposes of his creativity, glory and love with and through persons – human beings who contain the potential of being in God's own image. This must mean that any call to know God is a call to seek, serve and share with other human persons in the world at large. Knowledge of God grows through exploration with other persons who have to be taken seriously, along with their sincere beliefs about the world, religion or no religion. The church, therefore, cannot dictate the conditions of belief, but it can and must share the possibilities and promise of its faith.

It is the paradox of the church that the necessity of a continuing community of communities dedicated to the worship of God is inseparable from the constant betrayals of his gospel through the shortcomings and misunderstandings of his worshippers. My experience of this paradox was acute and personal. Persons whom I expected to be my allies in the pursuit of my calling to share in the knowledge of God behaved very much as if they were my enemies. Many of them certainly made it clear that they considered the way in which I was seeking to fulfil my calling was at enmity to true faith in God and his gospel in Jesus. Our animosity led to anguish on both sides – as I have tried at least to hint at, and as some of my critical comments no doubt reflect.

I have to make it clear, however, that I believe it to be quite wrong to regard this enmity between those of us claiming to be Christian as either decisive or definitive. Knowing or being known by God neither depends upon – nor guarantees – being right about God. One of the most important and practical messages I was put on to in the Bible as a boy was that phrase the apostle Paul picks up in his letter to the Romans (3.10), 'there is none righteous, no, not one'. This never struck me as a depressing put-down but rather as a splendidly encouraging piece of realism. In matters of crucial importance and worth, men and women never get things entirely right – and often we get them almost entirely wrong (at times even desperately wrong; in theological terms one is a 'sinner'). This is never, however, the last word. It is a realistic assessment of the reality of being human. We do our best in the light of the good news of the gospel, and God continually offers us help ('grace' in technical theological terms) to recognize what goes wrong and promises to see us through to becoming what he intends us to be – our best, most fulfilled and most contributing selves.

So in a bad situation, where other people seemed to be wronging me, and where I almost certainly was making some wrongly motivated contributions to the whole controversial and increasingly miserable business, it remained the case that the 'going wrong' was not definitive – it did not exclude the possibility of a positive way forward. People who fall out – even fiercely, even uncharitably – with others from within the same communities of faith do not define themselves either by the manner in which they fall out or by the beliefs they fall out over. If God is God, then he is infinitely greater than all this, and he is at all times at work to overcome the testy trivializations of our discipleships.

As the apostle Paul says (2 Corinthians 4.7), 'we have this treasure in earthen vessels'. Consequently we can live in hope with the paradox of the church, although it is never acceptable or even excusable. Christian disciples live in the hope that 'sin shall not have dominion over you' (Romans 6.14), but that is not an invitation to keep sinning.

Any committed believer in God with a devout wish to share the knowledge of God must recognize that one of the most persistent obstacles to evangelism is the behaviour of those of us who claim to worship him. When religious believers focus on their own defence they shut God up in religious beliefs. 'God' becomes the object of cults that religious people pursue. Religion is thus reduced to a human pursuit to be studied by sociologists; just one more influential, sometimes psychologically useful but as often damaging, pursuit of socialized human beings.

I have come to see that the case for atheism is very strong. However, it strikes me that a truly rigorous atheism is as difficult to pursue as is a wholehearted determination to seek the truth and purpose of the living God. If atheism is a correct response to the world and its possibilities, then we have to face the actual limitations of our human resources, both shared and individual. The human race has shown a persistent tendency to imagine and invent and so claim to have discovered 'God'. If we truly are all that there is, how are we to prevent ourselves imagining, inventing and so claiming to discover secular substitutes for God, like the invisible hand of economic activity, or the healing hand of science and medicine, or the deceptive, lavish hand of money-prosperity? Perhaps the rigorous practice of atheism would be the best way to clear our minds and apply ourselves to maximizing the potential of human living. Perhaps the divertimentos of religion keep us whistling in the dark, preventing us from making the most of what light, liberty, space and vision are available to us.

It is my considered decision not to believe this. But in writing this book I am very much aware that the option of atheism is a very real possibility. I need to explore, and express for myself, the understanding to which my experiment and pilgrimage of faith has brought me, namely that the goodness of God pointed to and lived out by Jesus is about the resources for being human which are open to us all.

Now that we are all so evidently part of one limited earth, interdependent and yet competing in a network of markets, communications, and shared resources, humanity clearly needs all the inspiration and guidance it can get to move us towards sustainable ways of living together. Christians need to consider how our understanding of the universality of God and the good news expressed in Jesus contributes to, and is illuminated by, this present stage of human existence. But to do that we need God's resources to inspire and direct our faith and we need to break out beyond the smothering embrace of religion.

The learning curve I have undergone as I reflected on my experiences of the conflict over God and the lightning has demonstrated to me just how ambivalent my relationship with the Church of England has been. My personal experience of the paradox of the church is best expressed as, 'too often, I cannot do with the church, but I cannot do without it'. I think that this is just something that has to be lived with. It means that as an 'insider' of the church I tend to have my views much affected by my interest in 'outsiders'. This does not mean that I have no concerns for my fellow insiders, but it certainly affected my priorities as Bishop of Durham.

I believe that the church exists for all – outsiders quite as much as insiders (Christ died for us all). So insiders should be supported and directed to this universal mission. This means that I have grave doubts about the predominance of the present emphasis on the maintenance of parochial life as it now is in the thinking and practice of the Church of England. We are focused almost entirely on meeting the personal needs of those who come to church – a small minority. Mission and outreach, together with a general policy not of maintenance but of engagement in the issues of society which involve all our neighbours are rare, apart from a few exceptional parishes. The gospel, like human life, is about far more than getting 'hatched, matched and despatched', with the very occasional attendance at a service for Easter or Christmas.

Historically, this dominance of the pastoral approach was established when the church became the ally of the state and the moral bulwark of Christian citizenship and civilization. Those days are now over, despite the lingering survivals. I am quite clear that the mode of the 'establishment' of a Christian church for all citizens as citizens has outlived its usefulness. 'Here we have no continuing city, but we seek one that is to come,' as the writer of the letter to the Hebrews put it (13.14).

When I took up the post of Bishop of Durham with its automatic seat in the House of Lords I did so in the spirit of Canon Demant, a Regius Professor of Moral and Pastoral Theology and a Canon of Christ Church at Oxford University in the 1960s. One day the University Convocation was arguing over whether to abolish the cathedral canonry chairs of theology and Canon Demant – who held such a canonry chair – routed the abolitionists in a short and pungent speech which culminated in the statement: 'I am aware that I am an anachronism but I defy anyone to prove that I am not a useful anachronism.'

As Bishop of Durham I was aware that I was sustaining an anachronism that was rapidly wearing out its remaining usefulness. Nonetheless, it was my determination to move out into engagement with society at large that led to the third wave of my notoriety when, setting aside internal church discussions of faith, I dared to address matters in the social and political sphere from the pulpit of a public episcopal event.

9 The implications of being carved in stone

One late summer afternoon in 1984 I was being taken around Durham Cathedral by a Canon Residentiary to map out movements for my enthronement service. As we advanced down the nave I heard the small, precise sound of a chisel striking stone. We turned into the aisle that runs alongside the south side of the choir and the high altar and there, seated by a tablet in the south wall, was an elderly stonemason. He was carving a name at the bottom of a long list that began with '995 Aldhun'. Aldhun was the bishop who moved Saint Cuthbert's body, with his community following after him, from Chester-le-Street to found the settlement at Durham. The mason had just finished 'DAVID' and was starting on the E of 'Edward Jenkins'.

I shook hands with the stonemason, who turned out to be both a son and grandson of masons who had each in turn worked to keep the stones of this vast ancient building in repair. (I was told later that he reported to his colleagues that he had met the new bishop and that he was a friendly man with 'a good firm handshake', which was encouraging.)

It was quite a moment – to stand there and look at my name being carved into the fabric of this magnificent cathedral that had served as one embodiment of the church for nearly ten centuries. I felt the great honour of becoming the sixty-ninth Bishop of

Durham: to stand in this line of continuing faith. I was conscious of the great responsibility of the charge, and yet I came away haunted by the ambiguities of that poignant image of my personal name in the process of being carved into the stone of that imposing edifice.

The making of a diocesan bishop in the Church of England is a long drawn-out process, even after the Prime Minister has received the letter of acceptance from the person concerned. The name then goes to the Queen, and after the formalities have been completed, Downing Street makes the announcement. From then on the person concerned is bishop-*designate*. He is then effectively treated in the press, publicity and church as the 'bishop-to-be'. Legally, however, there are further stages. First, the bishop-designate has to be *elected* by the dean and chapter of the relevant cathedral. This is now taken so much for granted that the formal election comes long after arrangements have been made for the bishop's *consecration*. This is where the designated priest, now bishop-*elect*, is consecrated to be bishop indeed and in sacramental office. After that service one is regarded as the bishop of one's diocese.

One more formality and one more service remain. The formality is that of paying homage to the Queen. A bishop in the established Church of England must be a sworn servant of the monarch. Finally, the consecrated bishop, who has loyally paid homage to the monarch, is *enthroned*. This takes place in his own cathedral and is presided over by the dean and chapter of the cathedral, as I go on to describe.

So by the time I emerged into the sunshine outside York Minster on the morning of 7 July I was the Bishop of Durham (and to confirm that fact, my stipend as Bishop of Durham was paid from that date). But to finish off the process I had to pay homage to the Queen. Indeed, the date of my consecration service had been set so that my audience with Her Majesty could be fitted in before she left for her regular summer break at Balmoral. In the week following my consecration I went to Buckingham Palace to be presented by the Lord President of the Council, then Lord Whitelaw.[1] I paid my homage to Her Majesty, swearing allegiance to her and her successors. We had a brief conversation, in which the Queen lived up to her reputation for being carefully briefed. I bowed the statutory three times as I withdrew and emerged as the legal and consecrated occupant of the office of Lord Bishop of Durham. There remained only one final stage to be gone through – my enthronement in the cathedral of my new diocese, which had been arranged for St Matthew's Day, Friday 21 September 1984.

The enthronement service is an ancient ceremony, historically one of some grandeur. It is the formal and public celebration of the new bishop's assumption of responsibility for his diocese. The formality and ceremony reflects the mediaeval relationship between two independent power centres, the diocese and the cathedral. The ancient cathedrals are separate foundations that are historically wealthy in their own right, holding their own lands independent of both bishop and diocese. The cathedral church is governed by its dean. The dean acknowledges the bishop as spiritual leader of the diocese but in temporal matters he is a guardian of the ancient rights of his cathedral. (The dean is the second most senior cleric in any diocese, ranking immediately after the bishop.) Hence the formal enthronement ceremony, when the dean of the cathedral shows the bishop into his episcopal 'throne' in the cathedral church of his diocese. (Although the word 'enthronement' has kingly overtones,

---

1 Generally this task was filled by the Home Secretary, but at that time the Home Secretary was Leon Brittan who, as a Jew, thought it more appropriate that a Christian colleague should present new bishops to the sovereign.

in fact both 'throne' and 'cathedral' are derived from Greek words meaning a chair or a seat.)

When I first came to Durham diocese, the dean of the cathedral was Peter Baelz, a scholarly and deeply thoughtful man who had arrived in Durham after more than ten years of parochial experience in Birmingham, some time as Dean of Jesus College, Cambridge and a number of years as Regius Professor of Moral and Pastoral Theology at Oxford. Although we were acquainted, we did not know each other well, but from the first it was clear that we were on the same theological wavelength.

The fuss over my *Credo* interview had already had Dean Baelz working hard on my behalf. At several points in the controversy, his splendidly balanced letters appeared in *The Times* and the *Church Times*. I much valued his quiet, friendly support. Early on in the controversy when, as I am now inclined to think, I appeared on rather too many radio chat shows and news bulletins, Peter rang me up to suggest both cheerfully and firmly that I 'go easy'. He told me that on one late-night broadcast he had heard me begin an answer with 'there is nothing *certain* in the Bible'. He quite agreed with the statement in principle, but pointed out, perfectly reasonably, that in the particular context it was unwise and made life for the likes of him rather difficult. Peter Baelz remained a valued colleague and adviser throughout our time together at Durham.

(One of my favourite memories from my first year as Bishop of Durham is of a phone call from Peter on the evening of Holy Saturday 1985, the day before my first Easter celebration in office, when the media were making their usual fuss. He rang to report a call from someone who appeared to have come across his number while searching the telephone directory for a Church of England contact under 'Durham'. A male Scots voice asked him how one should address a bishop. That, replied Peter characteristically, depends on how rude you want to be. 'Och no!,' responded his caller, 'I dunna want to be rude. I only want to tell the bishop that they're discussing the resurrection in all the pubs in Rosyth.')

Dean Peter Baelz, along with his cathedral chapter, was therefore responsible for my enthronement service. In an introductory note to the form of service that Dean Baelz drew up for this ceremony, he explained the significance of the enthronement:

> It is not only rulers and judges who sit to give decisions. Teachers often sit, professors occupy 'chairs', and someone 'takes the chair' to lead a meeting. So the Bishop's official chair, his throne in the cathedral, is a reminder of his commission to lead and to teach God's people.

I did not see the form of service until a couple of days before the service itself, when I had already worked out that I wanted my sermon to be some sort of 'Declaration of Engagement' about how I viewed the purpose and direction of my time as Bishop of Durham. I was very encouraged, therefore, to find how remarkably well the dean's introduction reflected my own understanding of my episcopal and apostolic call. In my understanding of the apostolic ministry – particularly as manifested by St Paul – the job of an apostle is to lead the faithful in their mission to challenge the world with the glorious possibilities of the purposes of God, as shown in Jesus Christ. The gospel is not a static statement, but a programme for leading men and women forward by the power of the Holy Spirit towards the kingdom and fulfilment of God's purposes for all.

During the enthronement service I took the oaths required of me as bishop on the Durham Gospels – the most precious book in the cathedral's possession, a manuscript of great splendour and beauty illuminated by monks thirteen hundred years ago. This meant a great deal to me. The book was a sign that the service of my bishopric was essentially about the good news of God in Jesus Christ who is 'the same yesterday, today and forever' (Hebrews 13.8). Thirteen hundred years is not 'forever', but it is an impressively long time and a reminder of the far-reaching purposes of God.

This returns me to the ambiguities contained in the image of that stonemason carving my name into the wall of the ancient edifice of Durham Cathedral. The task of a bishop, as a follower of the apostles, is not to preserve the practice of a religion but to promote the pursuit of a pilgrimage. We are back to that paradox of the church which I referred to in my previous chapter.

It has become increasingly obvious to me that 'the Church of England as by law established' has become obsolescent and trapped in its history to the point where its ability to lead its remaining members (let alone our neighbours at large) into engagement with the possibilities of the universal God pointed to in the Christian gospel is dwindling away. I cannot explain to myself, let alone to others, the depth and significance of this increasing sense of ambiguity and ambivalence without a thumbnail sketch of the history and legend encompassed by that long stone list carved on the cathedral wall.

The story begins with St Cuthbert and the legend that developed around him. Cuthbert, who died as Bishop of Lindisfarne in AD 687, was said to have come from Ireland, the source of the seventh-century Christian missionaries to Northumbria and Scotland. At the end of the sixth century, Pope Gregory the Great sent Augustine's mission from Rome to Canterbury to bring Christianity to Southern England. In the same generation, Christian missionaries arrived from Ireland to convert the north of the British Isles. The object of both missionary thrusts was to convert the various Anglo-

Saxon and Celtic kings. Despite the ups and downs of tribal wars, and Viking raids from the 790s onwards, these missions succeeded in establishing Christian faith, worship and ecclesiastical organization to such effect that Christianity became the officially recognized religion across the land.

In his youth, Cuthbert had been received into the Celtic monastery of Melrose, situated some forty miles inland from the Northumbrian coast, and north of the royal fortress of the kings of Northumbria at Bamburgh. Cuthbert's far-flung missionary journeys, his preaching, and a style that combined personal austerity with an affable approachability, gained him a wide reputation. In 664 he was sent to Lindisfarne to become prior of the monastic community that had been established there from the main house at Melrose. On Lindisfarne, a semi-island totally separate from the mainland when the sands are covered by the tide, the community developed as the central base for mission to the North East. By AD 635 it had become the seat of the bishops of Northumbria. Cuthbert continued his work as prior, but in AD 676, following a Celtic monastic tradition, he moved further out into the sea to become a hermit on one of the bleak Farne Islands. His reputation attracted many influential visitors – leading ecclesiastics, and the king and queen of Northumbria, who came seeking advice and counsel. In the end he was persuaded, much against his will, to leave his hermitage in AD 685 and become the local bishop. The job killed him within two years. He died in AD 687 and was buried by the altar in the church at Lindisfarne.

After the fashion of the times, Cuthbert's memory and relics were much venerated and many miracles were attributed to him. Eleven years after his death, in AD 698, the monks of Lindisfarne sought the permission of the bishop to exhume Cuthbert's coffin so that his bones could be gathered together in a suitable receptacle to be placed in a shrine in the monastery church, where his relics and memory could be venerated by the faithful. It is reported that when the coffin was opened, the monks discovered Cuthbert's body in a perfect state of preservation. The miracle confirmed Cuthbert's status as a saint. The body was wrapped in a fresh robe and encased in a wooden coffin that became the centrepiece of the newly con-structed shrine. The shrine proved a magnet to visitors and the monastic community became rich on the gifts of the pilgrims that came from far and wide.

A hundred years passed, and in AD 793 the north-east coast experienced its first serious Viking raids. A band descended on Lindisfarne, wrecking the monastery, and murdering and enslaving all those who did not manage to flee. The surviving monks returned to find St Cuthbert's shrine intact, and they stayed on for a couple of generations. But when rumours of fresh raids began to circulate in AD 875, the bishop and monks took up the coffin of St Cuthbert and fled. They wandered again for some twenty years, but then the Danish king, who was by now established at York and spreading his influence through southern Northumbria, decided to opt for Chris-tianity. He gave the group a home at the ancient minster church of Chester-le-Street, along with a substantial donation of royal lands to the north of the Tees, between the Wear and Tyne rivers.

Although legend puts the king's conversion down to the abbot's consulting 'St Cuthbert' in his dreams in order to settle a dispute as to who should be king in Danish York, the territory under ecclesi-astical rule provided a useful buffer between the two kingdoms into which Northumbria had split – the Danish (and now increasingly Christian) kingdom of York to the south and the temporarily revived Christian kingdom of Northumbria to the north. The com-munity of Saint Cuthbert, therefore, was set to develop into the Episcopal County Palatine of Durham.

Through the next hundred and ten years the fame of the saint spread, and the community amassed more wealth from kings, noblemen and pilgrims. Then, when the Danes reappeared to ravage the North in AD 996, the community picked up their saint and moved again. After sheltering in Ripon for a time, they set out once more on the road north. According to legend, they were on their way back to Chester-le-Street when a vision of St Cuthbert guided them to a rocky tongue of land set in a loop of the River Wear. On this superbly defensive site they built a massive Saxon cathedral to house St Cuthbert's shrine. Here in his final resting-place the saint became a centre for pilgrimage, and his community grew rich again on the offerings the pilgrims brought.

So Durham became the seat of the Northumbrian bishopric. With the arrival of William the Conqueror and the harrowing of the North, the bishopric was taken over by the Normans. The English monks were expelled, to be replaced by Benedictines. These annexed the two ancient Celtic monasteries at Wearmouth and Jarrow, and the dominance of Durham was complete. The Norman bishop celebrated by pulling down the old Saxon cathedral and building in its place a new and more magnificent church, so that St Cuthbert's shrine would be the noblest in all England. With extraordinary Norman energy, the whole impressive edifice was constructed in just over a decade. The first stones were laid in 1093 and the building as we still know it today was largely finished by 1104, when St Cuthbert's body was moved to his new shrine.

Thus it was that by the vicissitudes of history (including the Reformation, when Henry VIII's Commissioners established the Church of England's independence from Rome in 1544) I became Bishop of Durham. I was deeply impressed by the thought that my name was being carved into such a succession. I found participating in ceremonies recalling this history – such as the annual Cathedral

Commemoration of St Cuthbert on his feast day of 20 March, with its solemn procession to offer prayers before the saint's tomb behind the high altar – moving occasions for considering my own faith, calling and mission (especially when I was presiding as St Cuthbert's latest successor). But as I began to suspect when I first saw the stone-mason chipping at my name, this history of nearly fourteen hundred years was a problematic one to be engraved into.

If one is convinced that God is concerned with the problems of today and the promises of the future, there is a clash (which threatens to become a contradiction) between the call to give priority to now and the future and the world-view reflected in the story of how the community of St Cuthbert grew rich and endowed by Christian magnates to the point where the Bishop of Durham emerges as the Episcopal Count Palatine of the North.

As the recent worldwide celebrations to mark the commencement of the third millennium demonstrated, today people have forgotten the significance of 'AD' – the idea that we might be living in 'Anno Domini', the year of our Lord. The numbers are now no more than a generally accepted system for the ordering of events. As far as the modern world goes, millennia have lost their significance. The long duration of a way of thinking, or a way of faith – the extensive survival of communal habits or shared standards of morality – primarily indicate that these standards or ways of thinking are 'out of date'. In the modern world, long duration is more often assumed to mean obsolescence and irrelevance than indications of truth or lasting value.

Our modern understanding of the world and time has changed drastically from that of the ancient classical world of the Mediterranean that shaped 'Christendom' as it dominated Western civilization up until the seventeenth century. In that era the world was seen as unchanging, though full of 'changes and chances'. Christians would pray that 'amidst the changes and chances of this fleeting world our hearts might surely there be fixed where true joys are to be found'. The eyes of the faithful were fixed on the heaven of God's eternity. Their hope was that with the help of the church, the prayers and interventions of the saints, backed up by offerings to institutions such as monasteries, cathedrals and churches, a place might be secured in heaven. As life went on in its unchanging cycles of struggle with man and elements, the churches and cathedrals marshalled the prayers of the saints and the devout for the benefit of ordinary human beings, from king to peasant. This was not just superstition. It was a world-view based on one understanding of God who had been uniquely revealed in Jesus, woven into a whole way of life. The central focus was on power: the power to rule, the power to influence God for good, and the power to fashion some sort of order in this life and foster some sort of hope for a future and better life. Worldly power was focused in and administered by kings and emperors, and beneath them lesser lords and magnates, including Lord Bishops. In the terms of the mediaeval documents that still accompany the appointment of the Bishop of Durham, the kings were lords anointed and the bishops were lords appointed. (The documentation that assigned me exercise of the duties of the bishopric in 1984 described me as 'by Divine Providence' Lord Bishop of Durham.)

This is the ancient world-view enshrined in the imposing edifice of Durham Cathedral. I came to view events such as the nine hundredth anniversary celebrations of the laying of the building's foundation stone in which I took part in 1993, or the millennial celebration of the diocese in 1995, as simply reinforcing the church's focus on looking backwards. What has a millennium of history rooted in the beginnings of the 'Christianization' of Britain to do with God at work today and the shared pursuit of God's purposes for his universal future? A church so determined to enshrine nearly two thousand years of tradition – particularly a tradition that ignores the radical developments of the civilization in which it now resides – is nearly hopelessly weighed down in any attempt to reach out to communicate the gospel in the twenty-first century and beyond.

Such a church appears before the public as a mere survival – good for the occasional display of public pageantry, but for little more. I was particularly struck by one passage from *The Times* columnist Alice Miles as she wrote on 10 April 2002 about the lying-in-state of Queen Elizabeth, the Queen Mother, in Westminster Hall.

> There was a funny feel to the Queen Mother's lying-in-state at Westminster Hall. It arose from a disjunction between the traditional regal paraphernalia, the flag-covered coffin, the soldiers, the mediaeval setting and the bright arc lights illuminating the scene for the television cameras. It had the appearance of a film set. The past nine days have been acted out like an historical drama.

The Church of England is often complimented for its ability to stage the pageantry of a public service, but how often does such pageantry communicate any sense of a lively or current Christian faith? I remember a comment Dame Margot Fonteyn made to me when, as Chancellor of the University of Durham, she attended the annual graduation service in the cathedral at which I, the Bishop of Durham, was present as the Visitor of the university. As we processed out side by side from the service, Dame Margot remarked, 'That was a splendid occasion – and so well done. You could have charged all those attending twenty-five guineas a seat.'

What does the Church of England's gift for putting on a good production, dressed with splendid history, speak of? It does not, I fear, speak of a current preaching of a universal gospel. It does not convey a gripping engagement with either the public or the personal affairs of the average British citizen – who are, in any case, not citizens but subjects of an anointed monarch.

The coronation service is another mediaeval survival with roots running back a thousand years. The royal anointing, which takes place in the coronation service, has its precedent a further two thousand years before that in the anointing of King Solomon recorded in the Bible. For those of us who continue as members of the Church of England, we cannot avoid addressing where our backward-looking historical 'Establishment' has left us.

What is to be the bridge between a society formally united by being subjects of the Royal Lord's Anointed and a Christian community of ecumenical and lively faith committed to following God's anointed (in Hebrew the Messiah; in Greek Christ)? The 'Lord's Anointed', the Christ of the God who is for all, did not rule under a crown. He suffered on the cross. The implication is that God is not an emperor or a king but a servant who shares human experience through sacrifice and death. This is hardly the vision of Christianity that built the walls of the Christian churches of today.

I was not so clear then as I am now about the depth of this challenge, but almost instinctively I composed the sermon I was to give at my enthronement service under the pressure of the troubling image of my name carved into this historical edifice. Just as I had hoped that my interview on the *Credo* programme would open up Christianity to a world desperately in need of realistic hope, so I sensed that my enthronement sermon must address some of the miserable challenges of the present time and engage the Christian hope that, because God had become one of us, there might be a greater hope for us than mere political dogmas of either Left or Right.

So I plunged in. The result was explosive – but I cannot see how I could, honestly and faithfully, have done anything else. I was the sixty-ninth Bishop of Durham. I was being enthroned in a cathedral that had stood for a thousand years. As a simple believer in God as revealed in Christ, and a priest of thirty years service, I had to embrace the challenge of being landed in the ambivalent position of being 'by Divine Providence' Lord Bishop of Durham.

1. Commissioning photograph, Royal Artillery, Catterick, April 1945.

2. Shaking hands with the Archbishop of York, Dr John Habgood, after his consecration ceremony at York Minster, July 1984. © Ross Parry

3. Laughing with fellow clergymen, the Bishop of Liverpool, the Rt Revd David Sheppard (right), and the Bishop of Coventry, the Rt Revd John Gibbs (left), in the Bishop's Robing Room at the House of Lords when he took his seat, 1984.
© PA Photos

4. Recording an interview with Rosemary Harthill off Inner Farne, 1987. © Rebecca Jenkins

5. Filming with the BBC in the Judean Hills, 1990. © Rebecca Jenkins

6. Making an impassioned speech at the Easington Colliery protest march, 1992.
© Ted Ditchburn, North News and Pictures

7. Talking to a parishioner, September 1993. © Don McPhee, the *Guardian*

8. Alone in the cloisters of Durham Cathedral, Christmas Day 1993.
© Michael Scott, North News and Pictures

10 My notorious enthronement sermon

When I arrived in Durham in 1984, I came to a diocese proud of its mining tradition. Every July, on the day of the Miners' Gala, miners and their families from all over the county would gather for a moving service in the cathedral at which the colliery bands played and their colourful nineteenth-century banners were paraded down the aisle. I took up my duties as bishop in the month that saw the beginning of the worst mining strike to hit the country since the 1920s. The strike began in September 1984 and was not finally settled until 3 March 1985. It was a desperate and disturbing struggle, accentuated by the larger-than-life figures of Arthur Scargill, the miners' leader, who day by day squared up to Ian MacGregor, chairman of the Coal Board, and his backer, Prime Minister Margaret Thatcher, in the newspapers and on radio and television.

The strike was the matter of the day as soon as I started work at Auckland Castle that September. In the first couple of weeks I was visited by some local miners' wives who needed to talk about a traumatic trip to Sheffield. They had gone with their children to a demonstration in support of the strike. They went as a family in the spirit of citizens trusting in their right to lawful protest. They and their children found themselves in the middle of a vicious fight between pickets and police. They were deeply shocked. The police they had encountered were not the kind of law officers they were used to. In their own communities their policemen had always been regarded as friends and allies 'in all things lawful and honest'. The police they met on that picket line were 'from the Smoke' (bussed in from some big city, such as Birmingham or London). These enforcers of the law behaved as if the miners – the women's husbands and their children's fathers – were the enemy, and violence ensued. The women asked me: What can we say now to our children about respecting the law and the police? Their trust had been destroyed and their confidence in their place in the wider community shattered.

Soon after that meeting I had another visit, this time from the presiding officer of the Northumberland miners and a couple of his colleagues. During our discussion, the president, an elderly miner, said something like, 'Perhaps you could lend us a bit of your lightning, Bishop. If we could just stun Arthur and MacGregor – we wouldn't want to kill them, mind – we could settle the matter ourselves.'

At that time I was meditating on what I should say in my enthronement sermon. Since I hoped to use the occasion to exploit the opportunities of my position – anachronistic though it was – for the sake of the gospel of God in Jesus through the Spirit, who is for all, I could not ignore these people. Mindful of Dennis Nineham's remark that bishops were, generally speaking, generally speaking, it was clear to me that I must introduce into my sermon some specifics that brought the faith I talked about down to earth. I knew that this would probably cause trouble and that I might well misjudge things. But I had to risk it. My conversation with those members of the local mining community left me with a strong impression that they felt themselves trapped, pawns in the ideological battle being fought between MrsThatcher, through her agent Mr MacGregor, and Mr Scargill and his Communist colleagues who dominated the National Miners' Union.

The title of my sermon was: 'A Sermon on the Cost of Hope'.[1] I took as my text a verse from Paul's letter to the Romans:

> May the God of hope fill you with all joy and peace by your faith in him until, by the power of the Holy Spirit, you overflow with hope (Romans 15.13).

I began by saying that we could do with some hope right now in the North East. From proposals to use our region as a dumping ground for radioactive waste to the miners' strike, our society was distressed to the point of violence. Christians were taken up with bad-tempered arguments about belief; church members were more and more worried about financial problems. Everyone, at the time, was concerned about nuclear weapons and the threat that one day they would be used. Hope did not come easily.

I expressed the concerns I have reflected on in my previous chapter. Was this cathedral just a magnificent relic of past history, or a sign of power for the future? I gave a brief personal confession of my faith that it is in the very midst of the ambiguities of our ordinary, daily lives that God is to be found:

> I face you, therefore, as an ambiguous, compromised and questioning person entering upon an ambiguous office in an uncertain church in the midst of a threatened and threatening world. I dare to do this, and I, even, with fear and trembling,

---

1 Reprinted in full in David E. Jenkins, *God, Politics and the Future*, SCM Press 1988, pp. 3–10.

rejoice to do this because this is where God is to be found. In the midst, that is, of the ambiguities, the compromises, the uncertainties, the questions and the threats of our daily and ordinary world. For the church exists, despite all its failings and all its historically acquired clutter, because the disturbing, provocative, impractical, loving and utterly God-centred Jesus got himself crucified. Then God vindicated this God-centred way of life, love and being by raising Jesus up.

Hope did not come cheap. We could not expect miracle solutions from either God or politicians. Keeping hope alive in our world costs the cross. And if God goes that way, we can expect no short-cuts.

I went on to apply this approach to relationships between Christians. I was anxious to emphasize two things: that church relationships must not be exclusive, and that Christian faith should not be cribbed and confined by narrow dogmatism. A modern understanding of faith offered open boundaries between sympathizers of all denominations and none, in the exploration of matters of faith.

It was on the foundations of all this that I took my plunge into specifics. Since the following passages contain the matter that caused so much public debate at the time, I think it worthwhile to repeat them at length here.

This offer of freedom for newness and hope under the almightiness of God and through the down-to-earth presence of God is not, however, by any means confined to Christian churches and religious affairs. There is a power and a possibility here about hope in our present social discontents.

Here, again, triumphalism, absolutism and illusions have to

be got rid of if we are to find hopeful and human ways forward. The cost of hope in our society and in our politics is a responsible readiness for compromise. Once we are clear that nobody has God's view of things or does God's will in God's way, then it also becomes clear that to insist on one's own view and nothing but one's own view, and the whole of one's own view, is outrageously self-righteous, deeply inhuman and damnably dangerous. It is to set our inevitable conflict on course for destructive fights, which no one can win, through which all will lose and which could end by destroying us all.

Until we reach the kingdom of God, responsible, mutually worked out compromise will again and again be of the essence both of true godliness and of true humanity. Anyone who rejects compromise as a matter of policy, programme or conviction is putting himself or herself in the place of God. Yet Christians and atheists can surely be agreed that, whether there is a God or not, no person or set of persons from our human race is suitable for divine appointment.

Consider the bearing of this on our most pressing current social tragedy, the miners' strike. I suggest that there must be no victory in the miners' strike. There must be no victory, but a speedy settlement which is a compromise pointing to community and the future.

There must be no victory, because the miners must not be defeated. They are desperate for their communities and this desperation forces them to action. No one concerned in this strike – and we are all concerned – must forget for one moment what it is like to be part of a community centred on a mine or a works when that mine or works closes. It is death, depression and desolation. A society which seeks economic progress for material ends must not indifferently exact such human suffering from some for the sake of the affluence of others.

The miners, then, must not be defeated, and this must be the first priority. But there must be no victory for them on present terms, because these include negotiations on their terms alone: pits left open at all costs, and the endorsement of civil violence for group ends. Yet equally there must be no victory for the government.

This government, whatever it says, seems in action to be determined to defeat the miners and thus treat workers as not part of 'us'. It also seems to be indifferent to poverty and powerlessness. Its financial measures consistently improve the lot of the already better off while worsening that of the badly off. Its answer to civil unrest seems to be to make the means of suppression more efficient while ignoring or playing down the causes. Such a government cannot promote community or give hope in the very difficult days we are faced with. It cannot even effectively promote the genuine insight it has about the need for realism in what is economically possible. To win a victory over the miners is simply to store up trouble, not to reduce it.

And there must be no victory for 'us'– that is to say society at large in our various groupings, who by our trends, tendencies and voting set up the sort of materialistic and consumer society we have. There will be no new hope for the future if all we get is the end of the strike and therefore, apparently, a quiet life again and the assurance that 'they' are dealing with things. Our problems will not go away. We shall find hope only if more and more of us are prepared to face up to what is going on, what is wrong in it, and what might be brought out of it.

Therefore a negotiated settlement which is a compromise and demands of us all further work on the problem both of the miners and of society at large is the only hopeful thing. But how might this come about?

Might it be by Mr MacGregor withdrawing from his chairmanship and Mr Scargill climbing down from his absolute demands? The withdrawal of an elderly, imported American to leave a reconciliation opportunity for some local product is surely neither dishonourable nor improper. It would show that the interpretation of his appointment as provoking the miners to fight in order that they be defeated was false, and it would indicate that the government values the cost of hope as much as, or more than, the fruit of victory. After all, victory leads to more and more trouble. Hope has a future. But this would have to be matched by evidence that Mr Scargill, too, was not an absolutist but a compassionate and realistic negotiator who cares more for people and the future than for ideology. Without withdrawal and climbing down it looks as if we are faced with several people determined to play God. And this gives us all hell.

I concluded:

Meanwhile, whatever may happen in the immediate future, the direction of the life of any branch or section of the Christian church is clear. The direction is God. This is the God who has already paid the cost of hope in this confusing, risky, but potentially glorious and often enjoyable world. He it is who is as he is in Jesus, identified with our flesh and blood, ready to meet us through his Spirit wherever there is human need or despair, human creativity or joy.

What we have to do is to face up to what is going on, get involved in what is going on, and discern him in what is going on. His gift will be himself; his promise will be the growth of all that is human and his power will be hope. And in the midst of it all our anchor and assurance will be to worship him, to wait for him and to rest in him.

So 'may the God of hope fill you with all joy and peace by your faith in him until, by the power of the Holy Spirit, you overflow with hope'.

The congregation applauded at some length. I was moved, and in order to control my emotion I struck my hand several times on the pulpit edge. At least one paper recorded that I had 'conducted the applause'. I was well and truly launched as a controversial figure.

'I thought the man had no sense of time or place,' the Bishop of Peterborough, Douglas Feaver, was reported to have commented to the *Daily Mirror*.[2] In fact I had a very clear sense of place and, I would argue, a perfect sense of timing. As far as my episcopate was concerned it was now or never. As the sixty-ninth Bishop of Durham, being enthroned in a nine-hundred-year-old cathedral, I had to signal that I had a mission and a concern stemming from the gospel of the God and Father of our Lord Jesus Christ that was of current significance to the north-east of Britain in the autumn of 1984.

The media interest was intense and the fury it expressed quite considerable. I had, of course, given a couple of hostages to fortune. The most obvious of these was my careless description of the Coal Board Chairman, Mr (later Sir) Ian MacGregor. He was not an 'elderly imported American'. He was in fact proudly Scots in origin,

2 *Daily Mirror* of 24 September 1984.

although he had made his mark as a captain of industry in the USA. He had worked there until 1980 when, at the age of sixty-seven, he was invited to return to Britain as Chairman and Chief Executive of the British Steel Corporation. The accusation that he was 'imported' was to a degree true, since he had been brought back from the States to address the overweening power of the trade unions and reorganize the nationalized steel industry in preparation for its privatization. Union power in the steel industry had been more or less tamed after the management broke a protracted strike in the early 1980s. Mr MacGregor was then invited to become Chairman of the Coal Board and turn his attention to the powerful coal-mining unions.

I am now aware that back in September 1984 I had an insufficient understanding of the scope of the strategies that Mrs Thatcher and her government were working to on the one hand, and Mr Scargill and his followers in the Miners' Union were pursuing on the other. What had distressed me from the moment I came to Durham was the uncertainty and fear of ordinary people from mining families who lived in villages around me. I wanted to see the conflict stopped as soon as possible so that a decent longer-term solution could be found. With hindsight I now know that given the protagonists such a happy solution was impossible.

I had a sense at the time – and I am much clearer now – that the tactics adopted by Mr Scargill bore a good deal of responsibility for this. His perception of the situation was Manichaean or dialectical. He was ruthlessly opposed to his perceived enemy, 'the capitalists'. The majority of the miners and their families that I had contact with had no such desire for an out-and-out struggle to final victory or defeat. They were ready for reasonable negotiations and compromise. But they were trapped. Mr Scargill and Mrs Thatcher were mutually committed to a fight to the end.

Back before the Conservative Party came to power in 1979,

Nicholas Ridley, the radical right-wing MP, drew up a report for the party's policy group on the nationalized industries. It addressed the problem of how to counter any 'political threat' from those who were regarded as enemies of the next Tory government. The members of the policy group suggested that in the first or second year of a new Tory government there might be a major challenge from a trade union over the application of monetarist policies to industry, and specifically over wage claims or redundancies. The report identified the coal industry as being particularly 'vulnerable', any industrial dispute there being likely to attract the support of 'the full force of Communist disruptors'.[3] The policy group suggested that a Thatcher government prepare itself by building up coal stocks to a maximum, particularly at power stations; by making contingency plans to import coal; by encouraging the recruitment of non-union lorry drivers by haulage companies to be ready to move coal in the face of pickets; and by converting power stations to dual coal/oil firing as quickly as possible. The report concluded:

> There should be a large, mobile squad of police equipped and prepared to uphold the law against violent picketing. 'Good non-union drivers' should be recruited to cross picket lines with police protection.

Anyone who witnessed events in the mining districts between March 1984 and March 1985 will realize how remarkably the scenario followed that sketched out in the Ridley Report. Mr Mac-Gregor was carefully chosen in the light of this strategy. Ian MacGregor believed in a Darwinian view of society. It was his con-

---

3 For further details see *The Economist*, 6 October 1984, which reprints comments on the report from its issue of 27 May 1978.

viction that 'this world is not forgiving to those who are not com-
petitive'. His obituary in the *Financial Times* of 14 April 1988
described how

> Sir Ian saw the strike more and more as it continued, and
> particularly after its close, as a contest for the preservation of
> democracy. He wrote afterwards in his autobiography, *The
> Enemies Within*: 'The lesson above all lessons to be learned
> from that strike is that we cannot depend on democracy. It
> depends on us . . .' Sir Ian's view refused to discriminate
> between a 'collectivism'– like Mr Scargill's – which posed a
> threat to democracy, and that sustainable within democracy
> and supportive of it. The harshness of the choices he had to
> make form part of that judgement: but the other part had
> already been formed by his own Manichaean view of the
> world, a view which found its parallel in Mr Scargill.

Since I have used this word Manichaean twice, I should explain
it. The Manichees were followers of a prophet called Mani who was
born in Babylonia early in the third century AD. His philosophy was
very influential in Mediterranean culture for a time. Drawing on
elements from Christianity, Buddhism and Zoroastrianism, the cult
explained the problem of good and evil in the world by an absolute
dualism. There were two forces in contest: one was God and good,
the other was evil and darkness. God was light; evil was matter.
Mani taught his followers that humanity was a tragic mix of light
and darkness. Men and women could only free themselves for good
and for God if they would follow elaborate routines to free themselves from matter and lift themselves to a higher, more spiritual
plane. The opposition was absolute and the conflict total. There was
no room for compromise.

It may seem irrelevantly theoretical to reflect on the Manichaean aspects of Mr MacGregor's and Mr Scargill's respective attitudes to the world, but it helps to illustrate an important point. It is obvious, once you think about it, that people's views on politics and economics are shaped by 'world-views', personal assumptions about the values that ought to be promoted through political and economic policies. These perspectives inevitably imply views on human nature, human hope and human resources. Sometimes these views are systematically developed, articulated and labelled. More often they are taken for granted, operating through habit or institutions. But whether consciously formulated or not, they affect the way one votes, what one protests about, the priority one gives to money-making or whatever. Economic and political actions express our views on life – what is real, what is worth striving for, what one hopes for and how far we believe we can affect things.

A 'Manichaean' perspective which sees the world sharply divided between good and evil encourages one to take a hard line in both one's way of life and in politics. It is obvious that one must struggle for what is 'good' and refuse to compromise with 'evil'. Mr Scargill, Mr MacGregor and Mrs Thatcher all considered themselves caught up in such a struggle. Mr Scargill was fighting for the victory of workers' power and prosperity after a history of the oppression of the proletariat. Mrs Thatcher and Mr MacGregor were battling for market freedom and the prosperity it would bring to all those prepared to give themselves wholeheartedly to competition in the market. There was one way, Left, or there was another, Right. No compromise was possible between the two. In fact the Tory Prime Minister invented a new presiding goddess, TINA, who took the place of fate in her frequently repeated conviction that 'There Is No Alternative' to the free market.

The importance Mrs Thatcher attached to her confrontation with the Scargill-led miners is illustrated in the concluding paragraph of her chapter on 'Mr Scargill's Insurrection' in her memoirs.

> The coal strike was always about far more than uneconomic pits. It was a political strike. And so its outcome had a significance far beyond the economic sphere. From 1972 to 1985 the conventional wisdom was that Britain could only be governed with the consent of the trade unions. No government could really resist, still less defeat, a major strike; in particular a strike by the miners' union. Even as we were reforming trade union law and overcoming lesser disputes, such as the steel strike, many on the left and outside it continued to believe that the miners had the ultimate veto and would one day use it. That day had now come and gone. Our determination to risk a strike emboldened the ordinary trade unionist to defy the militants. What the strike's defeat established was that Britain could not be made ungovernable by the Fascist Left. Marxists wanted to defy the law of the land in order to defy the laws of economics. They failed, and in doing so demonstrated just how mutually dependent the free economy and a free society really are. It is a lesson no one should forget.[4]

The Achilles' heel of this argument is implicit in Lady Thatcher's splendid sentence, 'Marxists wanted to defy the law of the land in order to defy the laws of economics.' It was to a certain extent true that Mr Scargill, inspired by Marxism, had organized militants among the miners against the law and order of the Tory government

---

4 Margaret Thatcher, *The Downing Street Years*, HarperCollins 1993, pp. 377f.

led by Mrs Thatcher. But it does not follow that Mrs Thatcher's 'laws of economics' represented 'good'. Mr Scargill, like Marx and Mrs Thatcher, believed that economics governed human organization and that economic productivity was the one and only way to human thriving. In the dialectic of economics and power, Mr Scargill saw Mrs Thatcher as a defender of the wealthy capitalist oppressors who manipulated money among themselves in order to keep the workers on minimal wages that would ensure their compliance. He was fighting so that the workers could gain power to govern in order that the means of production could be used for the shared prosperity of all. From Mr Scargill's point of view the basic issue about humanity and hope was, therefore, who controlled political power: the workers who provided the labour or the capitalists who monopolized money.

This is, of course, a gross oversimplification of the vast ideological debates about power, economic production and the means to human prosperity that have raged since the publication of the Communist Manifesto in 1848. It serves to emphasize, however, that the things with which the Christian gospel is concerned – our views of life: what is real, what is worth striving for, how one endures and what one hopes for – are also involved in economic and political actions. In many ways, economic definitions of 'the market' have taken over from God as the purveyor of whatever salvation, prosperity and happiness can be available to men and women on this earth.

The struggle to 'get the market right' (freeing the markets) was therefore a Manichaean question – a question of right and good versus wrong and evil – for both Mrs Thatcher and Mr Scargill. Mrs Thatcher pursued victory against Mr Scargill and 'the Fascist Left' in the conviction that it was one step towards transformation on a global scale. Once no one was left to 'defy the laws of economics',

then all would be well. Mr Scargill threw his lot in with the proletariat; Mrs Thatcher threw hers in with the market – but both
philosophies fixed and limited the potential of humanity. Either
human beings were determined by the dialectic or by the market –
either way TINA holds the ring: 'There Is No Alternative.'

This is fatalistic, superstitious, a total abdication of moral responsibility and – I think I have to say – both absurd and stupid. Fancy
writing off the possibility of responsible citizenship or any hopeful
human collaboration merely on the basis of some theory about the
proletariat or the market! It is a measure of the self-preoccupation of
the Christian churches that ideas of the potential of humanity
should have been left to such unimaginative and materialistic
ideologies.

So I plunged into these arguments over economics, politics and
power for the sake of the people around me and for the sake of my
faith in the God and Father of our Lord Jesus Christ. I was not as
efficient as I might have been, or as careful as I should have been, in
following up the issues and opportunities that arose through the
publicity I attracted. But at least I was following my calling to be in
the midst of what was happening to real people for the purposes and
service of the God who – I remain convinced – is truly as he is in
Jesus: down to earth among us and offering a future of love to us all.

11 Bishops and politics

There is an old press photograph that evokes – for me at least – the turbulence and excitement of my first months as bishop. In grainy black and white my head and shoulders can be distinguished in a mass of other heads and faces of miners and police as I am making my way into the NACODS headquarters in Doncaster in the autumn of 1984.

As a result of the publicity given to my enthronement sermon, officials of the National Association of Colliery Overmen, Deputies and Shotfirers (NACODS) invited me to be one of the independent witnesses at the count of their upcoming strike ballot which was to take place on the Friday following my enthronement. It was to be a critical vote in the history of the strike. This was the union of the supervisors and safety officers without whose presence no shifts could go down the mines.

Looking back now, I think I accepted this invitation out of the sheer excitement of engagement. I am not sure that it was prudent or even helpful but, as I have already pointed out, my approach to my episcopal calling was to plunge into the middle of what mattered to people in my area and see how God might make use of me. So I plunged. I think the episode contributed to establishing a bond between me and many in the mining community in the North East.

Over the years I have been presented with four miner's safety lamps at a variety of NUM occasions. One lamp carries the inscription 'Rt Revd David Jenkins, Bishop of Durham, in appreciation of his services in the dedication of the NUM North East Area Banner'. I remember that dedication well. It was a melancholy occasion because that banner marked the end of the Northumberland Area and everyone present knew that the Durham Area too was on its way out (although no one expected it to fade away quite as quickly as it did). I spoke about the uncertain future and warned all concerned that they would need their great gifts of social solidarity and their traditional capacity for endurance, for they had to look for and build a different future – not for their mining communities but for their children and their own community.

The response from the floor was not particularly enthusiastic. Arthur Scargill, who was also on the platform, was moved to add another fifteen minutes to his harangue about fate and the future. But behind the scenes, some of the local leaders thanked me for stating the obvious. A few weeks later I was asked to address a 'closure demonstration' at the gates of Easington Colliery. It was like conducting a funeral service. I tried to speak about the possibilities for building a new future, beyond the devastation of the mine closure. As I left, the local NUM official told me that it was too early for him to dare to voice such things, but he thanked me for saying what needed to be said. It seemed to me that that was one of my uses – saying what needed to be said though no one wanted to say it yet, and acting as something of a lightning conductor.

It was impossible not to share some of the bitterness that these communities felt about being written off and forgotten (as not a few coal-mining areas still are today, despite all the community revival campaigns and programmes for renewal). I will always remember going back to the miners' club at Easington after the closure ceremony and the face of one the younger miners in tears of despair.

If capitalism requires the destruction of industries and the communities around them in the interests of the market, are we not wealthy enough as a society to organize a more decent transition for these shattered communities? There is too much bland acceptance of such human costs among the successful middle classes and well-to-do. Sometimes I wonder if it would serve the middle classes right if the free market in which we put our trust defrauds us of our expected pensions. Perhaps the shock would help us to get together as a society to face up to the real price of our self-indulgence and open our eyes to the appropriateness of some greater redistribution of wealth through taxation for the common good.

As I responded to these people I did not see myself as interfering in politics or dabbling in economics. I was concerned with a much wider perspective – one informed by my glimpses of God as revealed in Jesus and active in the Holy Spirit and his offer that all human beings have the potential to develop in his image. I knew that I was bound to get some things wrong as I involved myself in specifics. But I hoped to progress in realism and relevance. In all the risks I took I was guided by my determination to stick to a concern for people – individual, human persons.

This was the theme of my first speech as bishop to the General Synod of the Church of England on the morning of 14 November 1984 in a debate on 'Perspectives in Economics'. I was finding that my reputation for being prepared to speak out brought me contacts with many people who worked alongside the invisible in society – the poor, the troublesome, the overlooked. I got to know a couple of workers from a Citizens Advice Bureau in a run-down part of Sunderland, one of whom was also one of my priests. In order to prepare for my Synod speech I asked them to 'let me have some typical cases which show the effects of recession combined with the cuts in social security upon individuals'. They supplied me with three cases. I selected one about a family of four with a depressed father under treatment for taking an overdose whose two sons (aged ten and twelve) had to take it in turns to go to school in the winter because the parents could only afford one solid pair of shoes between them.

I stood up to speak in a flood of television light and during my speech I cited this example of the hidden poverty in 1980s Britain. The lights went off when I sat down, and a storm broke. The 'one pair of shoes' story caused an uproar. The chattering classes in London were clear that I had been taken for a ride. Such claims were clearly absurd in the modern world of Thatcher's booming Britain. In the forty-eight hours following my speech I was besieged with increasingly aggressive demands from the press – particularly the tabloid papers – for the specific name and address of the family concerned so that 'their story could be checked out'.

This was impossible to provide. The father of the family who had been persuaded to give permission for his story to be used anonymously, in order to highlight a wider issue, was deeply depressed and in no condition to withstand an assault by the massed British media. My staff and I tried to provide alternative illustrations of my point about the persistence of real poverty in Britain. In the same city of Sunderland, for instance (partly due to deprivation exacerbated by the miners' strike), the Mayor's Hardship Fund had received several hundreds of requests that year for money to buy children's shoes as winter approached. The local press were more understanding than the national media. Appreciating the point about the need to protect vulnerable individuals, a group of local papers selected a representative who, a few days after my speech, was taken to visit various families by my friends working at the Advice

Bureau. The local papers then published some thoughtful articles, but the national press was no longer interested. They had moved on from the foolish bishop and his naïve acceptance of the absurd 'one pair of shoes' story.

In conclusion, the broadsheets remained largely as sceptical as the tabloids, although the *Observer* did pick out one sentence from my Synod speech for one of its 'Sayings of the Week'. 'If acting on monetarist principles steadily increases the number of the poor and makes the rich even richer, then it must be challenged.' (However, the editor missed out the next sentence that 'it is no answer to say: but this is the only way forward', a reference to Mrs Thatcher's TINA.)

The whole episode was a salutary experience for me. It highlighted the need for sophisticated back-up resources, available at a moment's notice, if one was to communicate effectively in public debate, given the nature of our deadline-driven news media. I was never to get this side of things under control. I found many of the press and media people whom I met sympathetic as individuals and easy to get on with. It is likely that at times I risked too great a frankness, which was no doubt a handicap.

Nevertheless, despite largely negative press coverage of my Synod speech, privately I received many letters from people working on the front line of the sort of issues I was trying to draw attention to (social workers and the like), contributing from the evidence of their own experiences and urging me to continue exposing such things.

What I found most undermining and difficult, however, was the response of Christians to my ill-prepared (although not ill-advised) intervention – in particular Christians of the conservative tendency, whether in politics or religion.

On the Sunday following my 'one pair of shoes' speech (18 November 1984), John Selwyn Gummer MP, then Chairman of the

Conservative Party as well as a devout high-churchman and lay member of the General Synod, preached a sermon at the university church of Great St Mary's in Cambridge.

His sermon made a number of hard-hitting points in response to my outspokenness at General Synod which, from the political point of view, were fair enough. I cite him here because his words illustrate the fundamental clash between the theological assumptions of this brand of Christian traditionalism and my understanding of the theological calling of a bishop. He himself was conscious that he was addressing an issue of theology.

> Any one of us who comes from the Catholic tradition must hold the office of bishop in real respect. The successor of the Apostles is a figure, as Newman said, 'whose slightest word spoken *ex cathedra* must be taken very seriously indeed'. And one therefore ought to start with stating one's allegiance; for me it is summed up in that verse from the hymn we've just sung:
>
> > And I hold in veneration
> > For the sake of Him alone
> > Holy Church as His creation
> > And her teaching as His own.
>
> That is why what I have to say today is much less about politics and much more about the doctrine of the church.

The phrase '*ex cathedra*' is significant. Bishops when they speak *ex cathedra* must be right about God; because of the inevitable risk of any human opinion being wrong about the complex practicalities of real life. Therefore should a bishop speak of anything but God in the abstract he will dilute his authority and thereby betray his calling.

By elevating bishops to being beyond contradiction about God, Mr Gummer's argument neatly eliminates them from having anything particular to say about the down-to-earth problems of the world in which we live our everyday lives.

Thus he lays it down that:

> The Bishop of Durham is plain Mr Jenkins when he gives his political views; he becomes the representative of the Church when he reminds me of my duty to God and to my fellow men.

More specifically, later in his address Mr Gummer states:

> If the church speaks, it must be in a way that is incontrovertible as far as the truth is concerned, for if it is not, then the message will be lost amid the argument about the example or the reference or the facts.

And yet, the great commandment is to love God and one's neighbour as oneself. How is it possible to fulfil one's duty to God and one's fellow men and women if one avoids any engagement in debates about the use of political power and the nature of our economic responsibilities towards our neighbours and our fellow human beings around the world?

For Christians like Mr Gummer the overriding priority in Christian leadership is certainty. He praises his own diocesan bishop because:

> What he presumes to do is what only the church can do, which is constantly to bring us back to the terms under which we all live, and the terms under which we shall die. That is what he does. And as a result I can listen to him and be con-

stantly reminded of how badly one lives according to the Gospel; and never to think to myself that his purpose is any other than that of reminding me of Christian certainty.[1]

This fetish of 'certainty' is neither Christian nor biblical. The Bible is a catalogue of faithful wrestlings with uncertainties – all the way from Abraham 'going out not knowing whither he was going', followed by the sufferings of the prophets, building up to the desolation of Jesus in Gethsemane and so on to the struggles of the apostles and disciples of Christian mission around the world.

I have to confess that I find it almost overwhelmingly depressing that Christians should argue that bishops can expect respect only if they are 'generally speaking'. All the more so, because this seems to be a view widely shared among those in authority today in our churches and the majority of congregations over whom they preside.

Sometimes this attitude is tempered by an argument that, for those bishops with a seat in the House of Lords, there is an appropriate forum where ecclesiastics may offer religious council to law-makers. The prominent Catholic politician, Norman St John-Stevas, made this suggestion in a letter he wrote to *The Times* in the week following my enthronement sermon. His first principle was splendid and expresses my own views perfectly:

> The Christian religion cannot be confined to the liturgy or the private meditations of the pious. Christianity will not be imprisoned in the vestry: the Christian religion is social or it is nothing. It is about the relationship between human beings

---

1 Extracts taken from a copy of the sermon sent to me by Mr Gummer.

in the light of the teachings of the One who set the supreme example and became in very truth the man for others.

But he goes on:

> Second, the guidance given must be clear and unequivocal, but on matters of general principle, not on particular political applications, let alone party-political ones. If this is not done, clerical statements, far from clarifying the moral issues, establishing the common ground, and modifying asperities, will simply be seized on as additional weapons by the protagonists in the struggle.

Norman St John-Stevas' long – and no doubt kindly meant – letter ended with a suggestion that I might put my various mistaken defects of presentation aside when I made my maiden speech in the House of Lords.

> Then he will have a real chance that his sincere and spiritual message will actually come across.[2]

As it happened, I went through the ceremony of introduction into the House of Lords on the very afternoon following my 'one pair of shoes' speech. It was a purely formal occasion and I could not help feeling a certain sense of history as I looked about me. As I signed the Roll of the House I glanced up to see an aged Lord Macmillan seated high up at the back of the government benches. It was also the only time I met Lord Hailsham face to face.

My commitments in my own region did not allow me the time to

---

2 *The Times*, 27 September 1984.

speak more than a few times in the House of Lords. Early in 1985, however, I did speak during debates over the government's Transport Bill.

The government's stated intention in this bill was to deregulate public transport and open that market to private operators who would compete for business without the distortion of subsidies or the involvement of local authorities. The bill ran to many clauses. When I first read it, what struck me most was that it contained a couple of clauses on deregulation and up to a hundred clauses of regulation under the pretext of preventing any interference with free competition. The more I studied the bill and listened to representations from community groups and local bodies in my area, the more I became convinced that the upshot of this attempt to give local bus services over to free market competition would be to the disadvantage of the poorer sections of society, and in particular the elderly poor. So my involvement in the issue, once again, was because of people not politics. Besides, as I said in my speech, 'this bill is based on something that might reasonably be called a faith . . . it is a faith about the nature of our society and the forces at work within it'. And since my Christian faith obliged me to be concerned with all factors that affect people, I was bound to challenge that false faith. This point was not, I think, much attended to.

The party in power was clear that I was interfering inappropriately in politics. In February that year, a local North-East Conservative MP, Mr Holt, articulated the politicians' frustration when during Question Time in the House of Commons he went out of his way to criticize my attendance at a public meeting on the transport proposals organized by local trade unions. He complained plaintively that 'the public rally to be addressed next week in Cleveland by the Bishop of Durham is exclusively to do with buses and has nothing to do with religion'.

Mrs Thatcher, too, by this time, was displaying signs of irritation at the 'interference' coming from the Established Church. In her memoirs she wrote:

> Sir Richard [O'Brien] was not only chairman of the Manpower Services Commission which supervised the nation's training schemes, but also chairman of the committee to advise the Prime Minister on the appointment of a new Archbishop of Canterbury . . . In view of my later relations with the hierarchy, I could wish that Sir Richard had combined his two jobs and established a decent training scheme for bishops.[3]

Although I think that the Prime Minister was to a degree disturbed by the criticism aimed at her government from some quarters of the Church of England leadership, it was not my impression that she ever paused to reflect on the underlying motives for that criticism.

I only met the Prime Minister once. She invited a group of bishops along with the Archbishop of Canterbury to Chequers in November 1987. I was told that she had specifically requested that I attend. Apart from a brief and inconsequential chat over sherry, I had no direct conversation with her and made only the slightest contribution to such discussion as there was at the day-long meeting. (Later, reports filtered back through the usual gossipy channels that Mrs Thatcher had found the Bishop of Durham unexpectedly pleasant. As I related the events of the day to my wife, she commented that I had clearly been rather impressed by the lady.)

My memory of that day is that there was no real opportunity

---

3 Margaret Thatcher, *The Downing Street Years*, HarperCollins 1993, p. 31.

for serious debate. The Prime Minister talked most of the time. It seemed that just as the lady was – famously – 'not for turning', she was not much for listening either. The highlight of the meeting, as far as I was concerned, came when she was telling us how disappointed she was that we bishops did not seem to appreciate that her motivation stemmed from Christianity. Both Christianity and liberal market democracy, she stated, 'were about freedom'. At this point the evangelical Bishop of Chester, Michael Baughen, gently corrected her in his grandfatherly way: 'Oh no, Prime Minister. Christianity is not about freedom, it is about love.' Far from demolishing her, this comment scarcely interrupted her flow. I suppose we ought to have at least tried to open a discussion of the practical implications of the insight of faith that the love of God so informs and directs the service of God and our neighbours that it ultimately promises perfect freedom. Such a discussion might have illustrated the relevance and engagement of both our sermons and our public utterances, as well as offering Mrs Thatcher something creatively different to mull over; but it did not prove possible.

Reviewing my various attempts at engagement through these years, it seems to me that I never really got to grips with the dismissive argument that practical questions of social organization that materially affect people have nothing to do with religion.

In fact the fundamental issue is the scope of God. If there is a God, then that God must be the God of everything for everyone. If, moreover, God created people with the potential of growing in his own image, then human beings are superior to any limited and limiting theories and they cannot be definitively trapped in any human theories of determinism, economic or otherwise.

Criticism of my supposedly improper and illegitimate involvement in political and economic matters continued throughout my episcopate. My political critics were fond of pointing to my media tag as the 'Unbelieving Bishop' to add to my discredit. This label, originally designed during the *Credo* affair, looked set to be glued to my public persona for life after my participation in another programme, this time a discussion broadcast on BBC Radio 4 on the evening of 27 October 1984.

The discussion was a lengthy one recorded for a series entitled *Poles Apart* that was designed to gather people of differing views to debate controversial topics of the day. The producer assembled an interesting mix of some ten people who gathered in the library at Auckland Castle for the recording a week before the programme went out. I thought we had a very good discussion – relaxed, searching and honest.

The subject at issue concerned my views on the virgin birth and the resurrection. I was asked why if things were believable symbolically and God worked in history, a symbol in history might not be seen as 'real'. My reply was:

> It is real, that is the point. All I said was 'literally physical'. I was very careful in the use of my language. After all, a conjuring trick with bones only proves that somebody is clever at a conjuring trick with bones. I am bothered about what I call 'God and conjuring tricks'. I am not clear that God manoeuvres physical things. I am clear that he works miracles through personal responses and faith . . . You cannot have a religious view about reality and another view about daily life . . . I am quite clear that God has not abandoned reality and history after the first century or even after the fourth century, and therefore to insist that in order to be a Christian you have think in the way that the New Testament thought (still less that you have to think in the way that fourth-century

people thought) is simply a lack of faith in God. It is to deny God in history and to fail in our mission.

Re-reading this transcript of what I said, I can see that it was not all that easy to follow without the face to face communication. The phrase that stuck in people's minds was 'a conjuring trick with bones'.

The next day, after the broadcast on Saturday night, the *Sunday Express* led its front page with the headline 'Bishop of Blasphemy' in heavy type over a derogatory cartoon of me and a text lambasting my dismissal of the resurrection as a 'conjuring trick with bones'. When I was telephoned by reporters I tried to point out that what I actually said was that the resurrection was far more than a conjuring trick with bones – the exact opposite of what I had been quoted as saying. Only the *Daily Telegraph* reported that fact on the Monday, but by then the damage had been done.

I was subsequently told what had happened by a sympathetic member of the BBC production staff. She was so distressed by the publicity that she traced the path of events. The producer of the programme in Manchester, it seems, thought it was good and so put together a selection of extracts (since the whole was too long to be used) and sent it down to the BBC press department in London. They, too, were interested and made their own tape of snippets of those extracts. This was passed on to the Press Association who gave it (or a copy) to the *Sunday Express* which had to go to press with its article before the actual broadcast itself went out on the Saturday evening.

I repeat these details as an example of the technical difficulties that contribute to the risk of public discussion of vital and complex issues in the media. Of course, it is the way of the world that practically everybody (including responsible and decent Christians) will believe that headlines and snippets are a reliable basis on which to judge the truth of things. My critics have always said that the obvious solution was for me to stop running these risks. I would counter: how else are these issues to be raised in the wider public consciousness?

As the years went by, every Christmas would see an outbreak of the same type of fuss as some comment was picked out of my exposition of the Christmas stories; every Easter my supposed views on the resurrection would be revisited. What disappointed me was the almost total lack of readiness among Christians at large to take advantage of the opening this provided to push positive discussion of Christianity with interested people. I think it was on the third Easter of my episcopate that one of the broadsheet papers closed their correspondence on the now regular discussion of facts and faith at Easter with a brief editorial pointing out that for probably the first time in history the resurrection of Jesus Christ had been the subject of extended discussion at Easter in all the press across the whole country. And what had the church done with this opportunity? Increasingly dominated by various varieties of certainty-wallahs, they met it defensively as an attack rather than embracing it with faith and hope as an opportunity.

It seems evident to me that the view that predominates in the Christian churches today is that God has indeed stopped. This can be the only explanation for the common distrust of a church leader who acts on a belief that God continues in the midst of all the developments of science, the ambiguities of economics, and even in the confusions of politics and party through which people struggle for freedom and sustainable living.

I did not realize what I was letting myself in for as I plunged into specifics for the sake of people. Looking back, I see now that I did not concentrate enough on particular objectives or on finding allies and seeking to build coalitions that might have influenced the realism and governance of the Church of England. I just took the risks – immensely supported by the positive responses I met wherever I went, and by the friendliness of 'my' people in 'my' diocese. Face to face, it seems, I can share with people that I simply believe in God, but politicians and the institutional church are another matter.

12 Political dismissal and ecclesiastical cul-de-sac

My skirmishes taking Christian faith and theology into matters political and economic continued in a desultory way throughout my episcopate. Effectively, however, they were nothing more than a sporadic one-man guerrilla campaign. I received regular letters of personal support from church members, and when MrsThatcher made the 'cuckoo' reference in her speech to the party faithful at a meeting of the Conservative Central Council in Newcastle on Saturday 28 March 1985, which was widely taken as referring to me, several churches reported that they had started up 'Cuckoo Clubs' in my defence. Such support was personally encouraging, but I do not believe that my persistent enthusiasms contributed anything to bringing the church's involvement in modern society up to date.

As I have already implied, I came to rely on support from sources outside the church. One particular engagement that moved me very deeply took place around Easter 1988. That Easter Day I made some comments to a Radio 4 current affairs programme on the reforms the government was implementing that week with respect to social security welfare payments. Relating the bias of these reforms to other financial adjustments in the government's overall policy, I observed that the general tendency was to withdraw support from the poor while increasing the wealth of the rich. In my assessment such a combination of actions was 'verging on the wicked'.

These comments, broadcast at lunchtime on Easter Day, caused another uproar. I had not only once more spoiled the Easter celebrations for all good Christians but I had also called the Prime Minster wicked. The latter point was just not true. I very carefully said that the government *policies* seemed to 'verge on the wicked'. (I have never believed in making personal accusations about the motivations of individuals – particularly when I am not personally acquainted with them.) As for the charge of spoiling Easter – I thought that paying attention to the plight of the poor was a singularly appropriate connection to make on the day above all days when Christians celebrate the down-to-earth involvement of the God who is for all.

While the newspaper headlines screamed the charge of conservative Christians that I was 'anti-Christ', privately I was caught up in a deeply moving experience. In the seven days following that broadcast I received over one thousand letters in response to my comments. Nine out of every ten of these letters conveyed the writer's support for my speaking out. The majority were from people who were dependent on benefits of one sort or another, telling desperate stories of personal deprivation. A significant proportion of the letters came from elderly pensioners who had worked hard all their lives, including many who had served their country during the Second World War. Now they reported lives lived in constant fear – fear of the cold, because they could not afford to heat their rooms; fear of the bill they could not pay; fear of being a burden and of being dismissed as no more than scroungers.

I found those letters harrowing. They deepened my disappointment at my failure to get across the idea that Christian concern for the lives of these people had to involve 'political' engagement, and that wrestling with human problems and communal financial responsibilities was not 'party political' but rather precisely where God and faith in God comes down to earth.

However, the Church of England at large, particularly in its synodical structures, was not much interested in these matters beyond the occasional debate. Moreover, I was given little opportunity to concentrate on this aspect of my ministry because of the time, energy and attention I was forced to devote to narrow ecclesiastical issues.

Between 1985 and 1992 the Church of England preoccupied itself with a series of quarrels between what were tagged the 'traditionalists' and the 'liberals'. The chosen ground for the first of these contests was the nature of Christian belief.

My attempts to open up the possibilities of Christian faith to the modern world had led to determined demands for synodical action from those I have come to nickname the certainty-wallahs. The movement created some strange alliances. Catholic traditionalists sympathetic to Rome formed a truce with Protestant fundamentalist evangelicals around their opposition to me and their mutual agreement that the principal feature of orthodoxy (whatever elements it might contain) was that it was composed of doctrines that were set out with *certainty*.

This campaign was deeply destructive of traditional Anglicanism. The Anglican church has always held together under a belief that belonging has greater theological resonance than schism. The distinctive Anglican gift and genius that I had inherited and had come to cherish was that a combination of scripture, tradition and reason – along with shared worship, respect for the creeds of the early church and mutually recognized orders of ministry – made it both happily possible and freely realistic to belong together so that we could develop our faith under God in the name of Christ and through the help of the Spirit without having to agree on all details and all interpretations.

Now this fine tradition was to be blown apart. I had apparently served as a catalyst for wider explosions that revealed a church rent by such anxieties combined with such insufficient reservoirs of tolerance and mutuality that its members no longer seemed able to muster the energy and humility before God to continue to work together in the hope of going forward together.

The manoeuvrings of the certainty-wallahs came to a head in February 1985, forcing the Synod to hold a debate on the limits of Christian faith. Synod referred the matter to the House of Bishops, requesting that, as guardians of the faith, they produce a report on the nature of Christian belief.

Something had happened to the Church of England. Under the pressures of modern uncertainties and the decline of belief in any sort of authority or relevance for the church, Bible or Christian tradition, the appetite, space and readiness for exploration into faith seemed to have collapsed. While I was convinced that God is about everything to do with humanity, the institutional church seemed to be turning its back on open and enquiring discipleship and preparing to shrink into dogmatism.

I first came face to face with this state of affairs during that Synod debate of February 1985 and during the discussions that took place over the following year up to the production of the House of Bishops' report.

The report on *The Nature of Christian Belief* was presented to General Synod in the form of a pamphlet. The first two pages were taken up with a statement on the particular issues that had prompted the initial controversy – the virgin birth and the resurrection. This was elaborated by a more discursive exposition extending to thirty-nine pages, comprising seventy-eight paragraphs.

The statement was a masterpiece of Anglican drafting. The troublesome disagreements over the definition of 'correct' beliefs on the virgin birth and the resurrection were side-stepped in a carefully honed phrase, appearing in paragraph (3): 'as regards belief that Christ's Tomb was empty on the first Easter Day', and in paragraph (5): 'as regards the Virginal Conception of Our Lord'. The phrase was: '*we acknowledge and uphold this as expressing the faith of the Church of England and as affirming that . . .*'

The rest of the statement made it clear that the House of Bishops as a whole held that the resurrection was true and real, and that the incarnation was likewise real and true. The point of the carefully honed phrase repeated in the crucial two paragraphs was that it was designed to imply that it was possible for some to believe in real resurrection and real incarnation without the empty tomb or the virginal conception being held to be anything other than vital myths representing the gospel of historical resurrection and historical incarnation which was the heart and core of the Christian faith. By this neat but unsatisfactory compromise I and others like me were allowed to remain included in the Anglican church.

No one was deceived and so nothing was settled. The House of Bishops had managed to produce a formula to which no one could object sufficiently to feel inspired to mount a further significant challenge in General Synod – at least for the time being. So the explosive material that lay between the traditionalists' demand for certainty and dogma and those of us convinced of the positive necessity for open exploration supported by the assurance of faith was simply left smouldering.

Under the sense of dissatisfaction I felt at this outcome, I wondered even more whether the 'Anglican' way of tolerance and experimentation could be practical any longer in a church which had grown so frightened of the indifference of the world that it chose to retreat into its own (and I am sure *not* God-given) manufactured certainties.

The completed report came before General Synod in July 1986. The debate lasted several hours. I was the fourth person called to speak. I suppose that I made 'the speech of my life'. (The text is printed as an appendix to this book so that my readers may judge it for themselves.) According to some reports it was received with a standing ovation. Margaret Duggan, a regular and shrewd commentator of long standing in the *Church Times*, wrote:

> Inevitably it was the Bishop of Durham who stole the show in the debate on doctrine. While it was possible for even non-theologians to have reservations about some of his logic in the early parts of his speech, few people have ever spoken so passionately about God in that assembly. I am not sure that he had the standing ovation some of the media credited him with – most of those standing as they clapped him were hoping to catch the chairman's eye so that they could speak themselves; but his own evident emotion won the emotional sympathy of many of his former critics. He might not be sound on the Virgin Birth, but the fella believes in God all right![1]

The general consensus was that I had 'won' through. In 1994 Andrew Brown, marking my forthcoming retirement with a Profile piece in the *Observer*, recalled:

> The evangelical backlash against [the Bishop of Durham] came to a head at the General Synod in the summer of 1986. His opponents had prepared long and carefully . . . He routed them. His speech was a *tour de force* of passionate arguments,

---

1 *Church Times*, 18 July 1986.

studied with quotable insults and condescension . . . But it left listeners convinced that they had overheard a humble man wrestling with his God. From that moment his position was secure, and he was able to perfect the role of Bishop of Durham unthreatened.[2]

At the end of the afternoon, the Archbishop of Canterbury, Bob Runcie, summing up the debate, commented as he drew his speech to a close:

> While not all of us will, as the Provost of Southwark has said, recognize our understanding of miracle in the Bishop of Durham's divine laser-beam, I know that the whole Synod will be deeply grateful to him for his moving and personal explanation of the questions before us. Nobody can deny that he has set our debate, not for the first time, in the context of the doctrine of God. The honest offering of his meditation for the scrutiny of the Synod tells us much about the characteristics of Anglicanism.

This statement and the sympathetic reception of my speech in the chamber as well as that expressed afterwards in the press and letters sent to me lifted my spirits. I was encouraged once again to believe that there was real life left in Anglicanism and with it the hope of sympathetic sharing and exploration – in recognizably mutual faith – across the gaping fault-line between myself and the coalition of my fierce critics.

---

2 *The Observer*, 5 February 1994.

13 The conflict deepens

My hopeful euphoria proved unsustainable. No sooner was the conflict over the nature of Christian belief laid to one side than a second and disturbing confrontation arose over the issue of homosexuality. I knew that once the church engaged in this debate there would be little short of hell to pay. It is hard to conceive of a more emotive mix than one that combines questions about the legitimate use of the Bible and the proper use of one's genitals. We were set for a confrontation which was tailor-made to provoke those cries of self-righteous intolerance that encourage atheists and secularists to feel only too glad that they have avoided the degradation of religious superstition.

In 1987 the House of Bishops produced a report on *Sexuality and the Church*. A determinedly evangelical and fundamentalist clergyman seized the opportunity to prompt a debate, seeking the House of Bishops' endorsement of the narrowest possible definitions of sexual morality. The report started out on uneasy ground because it contained another unsatisfactory compromise. Hedged in cautious language, it recommended tolerance – though not quite total acceptance – of consensual and responsible homosexual behaviour between consenting adults, but only if they were laypersons. The report made it clear that homosexual practices were not to be tolerated among male clergy.

The church still has not resolved this issue. I am listing it here simply as the second example of a fudge on matters of belief and morality in which I was involved. By a good deal of diplomatic negotiation, the report was manoeuvred through Synod and temporarily out of the public eye once more. After much discussion in the House of Bishops, the Bishop of Chester (who himself belonged to the evangelical wing of the church) crafted a set of amendments to the original mover's proposals that slightly modified the rigour of a clause on homosexual behaviour but otherwise stressed literalist readings of the biblical texts on all other matters of human sexuality.

No one – myself included – judged it timely to dare to take the risk of raising the fundamental question at issue. There are indeed biblical *texts* which plainly forbid homosexual practices, but – so what? Biblical *texts* support all sorts of things, such as the creation of the earth in seven days (Book of Genesis), recommendations for the genocide of Israel's enemies in the Promised Land (Deuteronomy) and a command not to seethe a kid in its mother's milk (Exodus). Our modern scientific understanding identifies the sexual orientation of every human being as fixed at some point on a bell curve between homosexuality and heterosexuality, suggesting that physiologically some people are simply born 'more homosexual' than others. Might this fact not be relevant to our current decisions on sexual morality? That homosexuality should be such an explosive issue within the church is simply more evidence of the supposition that God's revelation has stopped.

I fear that the 1987 debate presented discomfiting examples of embarrassment blending with collusion and dishonesty in the behaviour of practically every mover in the process, and certainly including the bishops. The presiding principle was deemed to be that the Church of England had to be kept together. However, our fudge only postponed the inevitable showdown. Eventually a faithful church will have to meet the issue of truth and reality rather than hiding in the thickets of ecclesiastical convenience and religious self-righteousness. This fact was even more transparent in the third fudge that followed on the heels of the second (this was one I played an active part in promoting). I am referring to the long drawn-out negotiations over the framing of a Measure to permit the ordination of women to the priesthood.

The House of Bishops focused its attention on two problems subsidiary to the simple Measure to authorize the Church of England to ordain women to the priesthood. These subsidiary problems were deemed vital to getting the Measure through General Synod and passed by the Ecclesiastical Committee of the Houses of Parliament.

The first problem was to provide a secure space within the ministry of the Church of England for priests who were conscientiously committed to opposing the Measure and continued to be irreconcilable to it. The second was to ensure financial provision for those in the stipendiary ministry who would feel forced to leave the Church of England because they believed that they could not in good conscience continue to serve in a church which, contrary to long-established Catholic tradition, had decided to ordain women as priests.

I was in favour of the ordination of women to the priesthood (and so, inevitably, to their eventually becoming bishops) because it seemed to me a routine modernization of the church's ministry, reflecting the reassessment of the respective roles of men and women resulting from developments in society, within the family and the workplace. When I first became a bishop I assumed that the change would come in due course. It was only as I became aware of the attitudes and motives of the opponents to the ordination of women that I became an active promoter of the reform as a matter of urgency. Dealing with the subject face to face among my own priests and laity, I observed that the notions of the opponents were mediaeval and tinged with misogyny, and that they displayed symptoms of being neurotic.

The arguments voiced by the committed opponents to the ordination of women were wholly determined by reference to church tradition and/or to biblical texts. They completely ignored the many insights revealed by cultural developments in the relationships between men and women in the world at large. The more intimately I became involved in the church's debates on the ordination of women to the priesthood, the more I suspected that I was an active member of an organization with questionable effects on people and a very limited approach to the world at large. Too much absorption in church affairs is a damaging thing, and total absorption in church affairs is devastating.

I came to see the ordination of women as an absolute necessity for humanizing the church and broadening its perspective. So I set about actively using my position to promote the reform.

In political terms it was essential to produce a sufficiently attractive package for the protection of those conscientious opponents who would remain unmoved by the arguments in favour of the Measure. If this was not done, the waverers among the voters at General Synod who preferred a quiet life could not be relied upon to vote the Measure through. There was a significant group among the members of General Synod who were not against the ordination of women in principle but felt it inexpedient or unfair to press the reform at this stage. Even as late as 1992, therefore, there was a significant danger that the time would be held to be not yet ripe.

So the House of Bishops worked at a threefold proposal. It aimed, first, to produce a legislative scheme by which parishes would be able to vote to opt out of the overall legislation and declare that parish a no-go area for women priests. Secondly, there was to be legislative provision for that minority of bishops who were opposed to the ordination of women, protecting their right not to ordain women priests themselves. Thirdly, a scheme was devised so that each of the two provinces of Canterbury and York would enable one or more specially designated bishops, who were themselves opposed to the ordination of women, to provide episcopal care to the parishes and clergy that opted out.

Overall, the complete proposal had to persuade the members of the Ecclesiastical Committee of Parliament that the priests' terms of employment were not being altered to an extent that could be construed as 'constructive dismissal'. Therefore a properly financed scheme was drawn up to provide for stipendiary priests, should they decide to withdraw from the Anglican ministry over the reform. This was to be available for up to ten years after the legislation was passed and implemented.

After a great deal of pretty agonizing discussion in the House of Bishops, a Draft Priests (Ordination of Women) Measure was put to the General Synod on the morning of 10 December 1992 at 10 a.m. It contained detailed proposals as outlined above and authorized the ordination of women to the priesthood.

Under the blaze of television lights, the debate, with a brief adjournment for lunch, ran on well into the afternoon. I found the whole thing rather tedious. Every argument had been well rehearsed many times before. Privately, the Archbishop of Canterbury (by now George Carey) had asked me to speak, commenting that he would like me 'to make one of your speeches about God'. It was hoped that the vote would be taken by 4.30 p.m. The archbishop suggested that if I stood to be called to speak soon after 3 p.m., I might provide a suitable way to push the debate to its close.

In her book *C. of E. – the State It's In*,[1] Monica Furlong gives an account of a long interview she had with Dr Carey in April 1999. In discussing the archbishop's concern to 'encourage, renew and mobilize the church for evangelism', she describes his intention to bring together a group of evangelists representing the three major traditions of the Church of England (catholic, evangelical and liberal). His plans were impeded when he could not locate a suitable liberal. Apparently the archbishop had wanted 'someone with a flavour of David Jenkins about him – "someone who can speak with enthusiasm about a living faith in God from a liberal tradition"'.

Taking this along with the previous Archbishop, Bob Runcie's comment on my *Nature of Christian Belief* speech, I cannot help reflecting somewhat wryly that while both Archbishops liked to encourage me on the subject of God they tended to get nervous when I came down to earth. However, I could not but be somewhat touched and moved by George Carey's request.

Thus I prepared a speech and began to stand as asked as 3 p.m. approached. Eventually I was called and gave what I regard as the 'second speech of my life' (again, I have included it as an appendix to this book so that readers may judge it for themselves). I tried to say as simply and as forcefully as I could that it was our duty to vote as we honestly believed we should, and to trust in God to see us through, whatever the outcome. I was clear that my firm belief was that a vote for the Measure was the way forward into God's purposes. (The archbishop, too, had expressed his support for the Measure.)

The time to vote arrived. The archbishop advised the chamber that the vote must be received without comment. He asked us to stand for a minute or two of silence, said a prayer, and sent the

---

1 Hodder & Stoughton 2002, p. 161.

members of Synod out to vote by Houses – that is, bishops, clergy, and then laity.

The procedure required that for the Measure to succeed, each House had to vote by a two-thirds majority in favour of it. The vote came out as:

	Ayes	Noes
Bishops	39	13
Clergy	176	74
Laity	169	82

This meant that technically the Measure was through with a majority of two votes in the House of Laity.

As I had already pointed out in my speech, given the complexities of the two-thirds requirement:

> the result of our vote will be in any case something like a statistical chance. We shall achieve not the will of God but the opportunity to find out where he wills to take us, whatever the outcome.

In practice, the vote represented a very firm majority of the Synod as a whole, particularly on such a contentious matter.

Looking back now, ten years on or more, the whole affair and the fuss and emotion it generated seems to verge on the absurd. We were all so preoccupied with the church's affairs with hardly any regard for its mission. Few people outside the churches could understand what the fuss was about – and in my heart, neither could I.

I knew from personal experience priests in my own diocese who were profoundly opposed to the move to ordain women and yet were splendid parish priests, with many insights and gifts. I have to say that I was deeply shocked by the effect that the church's decision to ordain women priests had on several of them. It turned men whom I thought of as some of my most decent and efficient priests into angry, disagreeable and hostile *little* men. My observation of many incidents of uncharitable and unpleasant behaviour led me to the conclusion that the motives that drive religious people to such extremes are primarily psychological and neurotic in nature. I am perfectly aware that if you are, or have been, someone in authority in the church, you must not say something like this. But now that I am in my seventy-eighth year I feel that I must be free to say it, because my experience shows me that it is true.

Many humanists and determined atheists would no doubt argue that all religion is a defensive response to reality and so naturally develops various neurotic taboos. I would not be finishing this book if I had not wholeheartedly rejected the major premise of atheism, but I cannot ignore the striking evidence provided by the conflict over the ordination of women (as well as, indeed, by many religious responses to questions of sexuality, not least homosexuality) that attitudes among church people frequently display symptoms which appear to justify the suspicion and dismissal of religion. What religious people claim to believe about God seems too often to make them smaller and more shallow human beings, rather than enlarging and deepening their humanity.

I cannot but wonder now whether all the fuss – and especially the elaborate precautions to protect everybody's conscience, however malformed – was decent or proper.

I am certain that the ordination of women to the priesthood (and eventually to the episcopate) is of quite immense importance to the future of the church and its mission. Once we can free ourselves from the continual sapping of the church's energies by the 'third force' in the no-go areas that we have created, and women are freely accepted (and so become equally open to criticism as their male colleagues), then something of the greatest importance will develop in the church. For the last ten years, however, we have all been greatly handicapped. Ordained women suffer improper discourtesies. They continue to be restricted from freely sharing their gifts and are hindered in making their literally vital contribution to the life of the church. But for the time being we must live with the consequences of the serious misjudgement that I, along with many others, made about the likely course of things if we simply implemented the provisions in good faith. I certainly never anticipated that many good Christian priests would dig in and fend off all attempts at co-operation once people had had a year or two to get used to the reality of women priests.

Today, however, attitudes if anything seem to have hardened. By establishing a second structure of opters-out with its own bishops, we have created a divisive and self-centred 'church within a church'. As I write there is pressure to set up a 'Third Province', a third province of the Church of England, beyond those of Canterbury and York, in which all irreconcilable Catholic certainty-wallahs may take refuge. Ominously the promoters of this Third Province have been joined by some prominent evangelical fundamentalists. This indicates that the basic issue is not Bible or pope, but the right to preserve an enclave of exclusive certainty on selected matters of dogma and textual interpretation.

The self-protective nature of this obsession for certainty among the leaders and members of the churches seems to take precedence over any sense of calling to plunge into the uncertainties and challenges of the world. This cautious and withdrawn attitude has been underlined, in the summer of 2002, by reactions to the appointment of Rowan Williams, the Archbishop of the Church in Wales, as Archbishop of Canterbury. Evangelicals warned via a newpaper headline that 'Williams in Canterbury would split the Church'.

The evangelicals claimed that Dr Williams' support for the ordination of homosexuals flew 'in the face of Holy Scripture' and would lead to the split in the Anglican Communion only narrowly averted by Dr Carey four years ago. The signatories of an open letter of protest sent to Tony Blair and Dame Elizabeth Butler-Sloss, the chairwoman of the Crown Appointments Commission, protested that Dr Williams had admitted ordaining a man who he knew had a homosexual partner. They wrote that 'such actions and views fly in the face of the clear teaching of Holy Scripture'. They continued, 'Rowan Williams would not have the confidence of the vast majority of Anglicans in the world, who are now in the Third World and who, as loyal Anglicans, take the Holy Scriptures as their supreme authority. His appointment would lead to a major split in the Anglican Communion.'[2]

Note the reference to 'flying in the face of the clear teaching of Holy Scripture' as just one current example of the attempts to use biblical texts as if they were clubs that can beat any rational argument into submission.

In the same few weeks rumours emerged of moves to revive some form of heresy trials for 'atheist' clergy. *The Daily Telegraph* reported:

Plans for the special tribunals, which critics fear will lead to 'witchhunts' against liberal clergy, have been drawn up by a committee of the House of Bishops. The tribunals, to be held in private, will hear cases involving breaches of 'doctrine, ritual and ceremonial'.

Clergy who deny the doctrine of the Trinity or the Incarna-

---

2 *The Times*, 21 June 2002.

tion, or who proclaim atheistic beliefs from the pulpit, could face charges, as could those who fail to wear the required vestments during the services.

One traditionalist, Margaret Brown, who is the present chairman of the Committee for promoting a Third Province, a synod member from Chichester, is threatening revolt unless the Committee adheres to the historical creeds and the Thirty-Nine Articles, the doctrinal formulae adopted by the church in the sixteenth century. Another, Peter Bruinvels, a Church Commissioner, said, 'at the moment it is impossible to reach consensus, with traditionals and liberals evenly split as to what really constitutes an offence and how serious it is. For example, some of us believe that the wearing of vestments during communion services is non-negotiable, but others totally disagree.'[3]

So the battle is to be joined on such absolutely vital matters to world mission such as what vestments are proper to the celebration of the eucharist! All this reminds me of what an animal ethologist once told me about chimpanzees. When a troupe get into a tizzy over some outside threat or some inter-troupe argument about bananas, they calm themselves down by turning their backs on the world and picking nits off one another.

It is hard to resist being driven to despair by the ways in which those now prominently active in the official churches – and more particularly in the Church of England – seek to enforce impossible and undesirable restraints on belief and behaviour in the name of the God and Father of our Lord Jesus Christ. Such attempts come perilously close to providing the evidence that the atheists, the

---

3 *The Daily Telegraph*, 27 July 2002.

agnostics and the generally indifferent are right. There *is* no God. How can he exist if he is reflected in a God-squad that is so neurotic, arbitrary, incredible and demanding – and so completely out of touch with any world in which ordinary individuals today have their being, pursue their hopes and die their deaths?

Throughout my ups and downs as Bishop of Durham, when under some particularly negative pressure (or when undermined by tiredness resulting from my own stupidity in failing to control my diary), I always found my ultimate personal refuge in the protective slogan 'Even the church cannot keep a good God down.' Writing this book has led me to face the unhappy rider, 'Is that truly so?'

As might be expected in any pilgrimage of faith, it is when one is near to despair that one stands on the verge of discovering something renewing and exciting about God – who in Jesus himself experienced the near despair of Gethsemane and the cross. And so, as I reached the point of wondering how I could finish this book – or even if I should finish it – I realized that the very writing of it had reminded me of something that I have always known. Even more encouragingly, it had brought me to recognize something I had never thought of with any conscious clarity before. I believe that these two ideas lead me into a positive and realistic continuation of my way of faith. It is therefore with these two themes that I shall bring this book to an end.

14 The sevenfold cord of faith

At the end of July 1978 I was attending the Lambeth Conference of Bishops of the Anglican Communion at the University of Kent at Canterbury under the Presidency of Donald Coggan, then Archbishop of Canterbury. I was one of the theological consultants. Much of the time the weather was not good, and the university is situated on some rather blustery hills on the edge of the city. One afternoon I was walking on my own in the rain after what I thought had been one more than usually depressing session on a largely unexciting agenda. As I was walking on with my head into the wind I had one of those thoughts which seem from time to time to come unbidden into my head. What the thought said was: 'This is serious, I may well have to resign my orders.' A bit further on another message came out: 'Jenkins!' (a throwback to my schooldays and time in the army, when I was always addressed by authority by my surname alone.) 'To resign your orders would be to take the Church of England far too seriously.' This was shortly followed by an amended version: 'To resign your orders would be to take the Church of England – and yourself – far too seriously.' I am not clear about the source of these messages, but the lonely walk on the hillside in the rain has remained with me ever since.

Recalling this has shown me that in struggling to set down as realistically as I can what I have experienced and learned in my ten years as Bishop of Durham I have nearly fallen into the trap of taking both myself and the Church of England too seriously. So I have become as preoccupied with the church as are all those whom I have been calling in question. Thus I am complaining of my difficulties and disputes and forgetting the obvious way to go on.

God has not called me (or anyone else) to be turned in on myself and the church. The calling of God is to be turned outwards for the service of his future for the world. This is what I have 'always known ever since I thought about those matters' to which I referred at the end of the last chapter. This is a reassertion of the calling of which I was first aware when, as I set out in the first page of this book 'I was told . . . that Jesus showed that God was for me. It was made clear to me that God was for me, because God is for all, because God is love.' That is the heart of my faith and that is what has remained with me ever since and is now renewed in me as I look back over the struggles which I have endured and enjoyed.

Renewing this confession of my faith reminds me and reveals to me that faith in God does not depend upon the church but on God himself. This is the liberation of faith. Of course the church cannot keep a good God down – because God does not rely upon the church to kindle faith. He does it himself, with some input from 'the church' in its broadest sense as an auxiliary or occasioning aid.

With this understanding of the nature of faith in the living God, to be dominated by, and trapped in, worrying about the church is nearly as bad as trying to retain links with the church while giving up all sense of the transcendent reality of God. Both are sad and unrealistic failures of faith. The quarrelling of the certainty-wallahs reduces the church to a set of authoritarian sects quarrelling about whose set of authorities and interpretations are really true and faithful to God. The very idea and hope of God is almost hopelessly compromised by such conflicts. On the other hand it is equally a mistake and failure of faith to take refuge in the idea that comforting – and even inspiring – memories of Christian faith can be kept alive by reflecting on the 'Sea of Faith' over which floats a spiritual version of Alice in Wonderland's Cheshire Cat, where the fading smile or grin remains when the body has utterly evaporated.

Both these approaches abandon the reality and force of faith. On the one hand internecine quarrels about God encourage atheism. On the other hand dissolving God into the echoes of purely human morality, aesthetics and longings is atheism. But faith knows that God is, that he is decisively (but not exclusively) as he is in Jesus, and so he is the hope of the future of all. This is the hope of the future which biblical faith, prophetic faith and the faith of the disciples through Jesus in the Spirit maintains and sustains. As such it is always the heart of the pilgrimage of faith. This is a very risky business. But God is love and love requires freedom in order that it may be received and freedom in order that it may be developed and shared. So faith in God is basically a personal matter of encounter, response and pilgrimage, but it is not individualistic. Faith is not a product or a set of beliefs sustained by authorities ecclesiastical or textual. It is a personal pilgrimage in company – the companions of the way of faith being those kept and maintained by God in the Spirit.

To bring this down to earth as something practical, experiential and existential – and to explain how I see the liberation of faith from the lines taken up by, and the quarrels of, the churches – I need to set out how I have developed an understanding of a sevenfold cord of ideas and experiences. These constitute the sustaining cord of faith which I share with my companions in the networks of faith in, and worship of, God.

The first strand is my initial encounter with the group of Christian men and boys (my local Crusader Class) with whom I shared the simplicity about Jesus showing me that God was for me because God was for all from which I started this book. What then developed was a whole series of meetings, formal and informal, rummaging around in the Bible together to see where this simplicity of faith came from and where it was leading. Doubtless this was a rather unique and blessed route, for although the leaders and keen members were very simple and direct believers in the truths of God as they believed them to be reflected through the Bible, and were deeply devoted to their understanding of God in Christ through the Spirit, the atmosphere and content of our meetings was free, searching and encouragingly enthusiastic. I have to say that I too often do not now recognize this simple and unaffected approach of seriousness and reality, combined with enthusiasm and openness, in the way many of the fundamentalist groups or crusading catholics now seem to engage in controversy and conflict.

I must have been very fortunate because, towards the end of my schooldays, when we were into the Second World War, much of my last summer at school was spent at a Harvest Camp in Buckinghamshire. There I went to holy communion on Sundays and became acquainted with an enthusiastic Anglo-Catholic curate who introduced me to what I can only call the devout mysteries of the eucharist. Once again, no prickliness went with the instruction I received – just enthusiastic devoutness.

So I simply grew into experiences of communities of faith, devotion and lively hope focused in one case on the Bible and in the other on the sacraments. It was not until much later that I got dragged into sectarian quarrels arising between the two traditions.

The second strand in my cord is what I came to learn about Jesus in his relation to God. I soon picked up from the Bible the intimate relationship between Jesus and God, the meaning and mystery of his suffering and the way in which, in their own ways, both Paul and the author of the Fourth Gospel set out the absolute reality of this intimate relationship. I found the Lord's Prayer and the hope of the eventual kingdom of God where his love would be all in all and shared by all, very powerful and promising.

I have to use a clumsy word here and speak of the amazing 'universalizability' which developed in the earlier proclamation and recruiting of the faith. The earliest statement of this is the summary in Paul's letter to the Galatians: *'There is neither Jew nor Greek, there is neither bond nor free, there is neither male nor female, for ye are all one in Christ Jesus'* (Galatians 3.28). You could not get more all embracing than that. This universality is reinforced at the end of the Gospels of Matthew and Luke (see Matthew 28.19ff. and Luke 24.47). It is stated again at the beginning of Acts (1.8), implied in the gift of the Spirit at Pentecost and discovered in actual practice through the whole thrust of the story-telling in Acts. This universalizability is what we have to rediscover for the future of faith, church and gospel for today and into the third millennium.

The dynamic and power of this human pursuit of universalizability with a view to the future of all is particularly and peculiarly focused in the central model of God which Christian faith has been inspired to develop – that of God as Holy Trinity. It is very important in a universe of process and change to be absolutely clear that this icon of God as Holy Trinity is not a metaphysical theory or map of the details of the mystery of God's being. It is an image or metaphor, or reflection of the internal dynamic of God as Love.

God as ultimate origin and source of all is – as 'the Father' – greater than great: his own mystery.

But this does not remove him from our most close and intimate relationship with him. For he *is* love – so much so that it is not the contradiction of his essential being but the most definitive expression of it within the processes of the universe that he should become a human being – one of us – in and as Jesus. This is the demonstration that he is – literally indeed and in doing – more loving than love.

All this is not beyond our practical understanding and our personal and collaborative receiving because this one and the same and only God expresses the dynamic of his love in being also, and at one and the same time and eternity, the Holy Spirit who is closer than close; for he dwells within us, in the deepest and most intimate depths of our being. He is also the link between us as human beings and is immanently, perpetually and purposefully at work in the world for the one purpose that God has as his very being – the fulfilment of his love in and with the future of all.

The Holy Trinity and the universalizability of our Christian understanding of God are, I believe, absolutely dynamic and vital clues to this prospect for the future.[1]

My third strand has been – and continues to be – my encounters with lively church-members, fellow disciples and many seekers, hangers-on and followers in hope of faith in my travels around the world. My four years with the World Council of Churches were particularly rich in this, but my youthful encounters with fellow Christians in India and my continuing travels since my WCC years,

---

1 For my more detailed wrestling with the church's development of faith in the Holy Trinity see lectures 7 and 8 in *The Glory of Man* (1966 Bampton Lectures), SCM Press 1967 and also chapters 6 and 10 in *The Contradiction of Christianity*, SCM Press 1976.

including the wider variety of people I met as bishop, have greatly strengthened my experiential conviction that God is around and can be found in down-to-earth ways in his pursuit of his universal purposes of love. One notable example of these many encounters which always remains with me is when I was on a trip for the WCC to Java in the early 1970s. The general situation was tense because struggles were continuing between Communist guerrillas and the government. I was spending a day at a Christian seminary outside Surabaya.

Christian pastors and theologians had come together for their annual conference from all over Indonesia. We were discussing mission and the modern world, not least because of the Communist and Marxist aspects with which Indonesia was struggling at the time. The conference had to be conducted in Indonesian as few spoke English (or American) fluently enough to be happy with anything else. So I was interpreted by a seminary professor from Sulewesi who had taken his doctorate in the US. The first thing that struck me was the relaxed attitude to time. I would make a point or two in English. He would have a discussion with me about it. Then he would translate it. Then he would have a discussion with the audience, making the odd note in English on the blackboard. Then he would have a discussion with me out of which I moved on to further remarks and the process was repeated. Nobody bothered about the timetable, and we broke for lunch at a convenient moment.

In the afternoon the ice was broken and many of the participants were quite ready to join the discussion in what I found was quite adequate English. But for me the really moving thing was to discover that we were clearly on the same basic wavelength of faith. I could not doubt that they knew something about the same God and Father of Jesus in the Spirit as I did. It was the relaxed and patient discussion which was so refreshing and revealing. It developed with people whose villages and towns were not far from, or free from, skirmishes and massacres. I have had many other similar discussions in many parts of the world. What I have learned – but regret that I have largely lost the habit of practising in the stress of life as a diocesan bishop – was the importance of taking time to let the human spirit, and therefore the Spirit of God, have a chance to emerge and be shared. This is closely related to the concept of 'revelation takes time' which I shall discuss in my concluding remarks. I shall not bring this book to a conclusion, it will just stop. For in faith, as yet, we reach no end.

The fourth strand is absolutely vital but so intimate and precious that I am going simply to refer to it. It is the amazing love of my wife Mollie and our four very varied children. Mollie and I are into our fifty-third year of marriage. Her courage, steadfastness and affectionate and enduring love are beyond description and evaluation. I have tried to reciprocate it but I know I have not emulated it. I just record this here in thanksgiving to God.

The fifth strand is made up of the resonances of worship and the excitements of intellectual controversy. Both have aroused reflections in me about new excitements and possibilities, discoveries of things I never knew or which I had never previously formulated and the general illumination and *enlargement* which has continued to accompany all this. Intellectual investigation and exploration, pursued by rigorous questioning and disciplined investigation, is not barren but highly creative and promising. There is a 'more' to investigate, a 'more' to discover and a 'more' to trust in.

A very important and practical biblical text for me is the verse at the beginning of the letter to the Hebrews, chapter 11. (The whole of Hebrews 10.38 to 12.2 on faith is of primary hopeful importance and engagement for me.) The verse in the Authorized Version reads:

'*Now faith is the substance of things hoped for and the evidence of things not seen.*' The Greek, I think, is more telling and indicates that faith provides the substantial evidence (as I believe by existential encounters) in our belief in and the service of God. As we go on in faith we then find sound grounds for believing in 'things not seen' because the testings of experience, and the obedience invited by faith, bring one into situations where something of the assurance of being known by God breaks in. There is therefore both substance given for what faith hopes for and evidence provided of something not seen but inwardly experienced and mutually shared.

The sixth strand is a range of continuing personal experiences which I recognize cannot necessarily prove anything to anyone else but which mean, in one way or another, everything to me. A regular feature of these experiences occurs from time to time when I am celebrating the eucharist. My liturgical prayers are transformed for me into an experience that I can only describe as 'there is a praying' – God, everybody and everything is somehow caught up into this particular moment of personal and communal worship, informed by the tradition of God in Jesus Christ. Then there are moments of wonder and stillness which would require poetry to express if I could write about them at all. I find them resonating with nature mystics such as the atheist Richard Jefferies when he describes the transfiguration of a field as he was watching it in the spring.

Just to risk one example: I have a vivid memory of walking in the wooded grounds of Auckland Castle in the spring of 1985 when all the fuss that I have been recording in this book was at its height. I was trying simply to be quiet and observant (I find it very difficult to stop thinking). I suddenly noticed – for I was going up hill gazing at the ground – that I had in fact walked into a patch covered with small violets whose colour deepened as I attended to them. Looking up I saw that the whole hillside, trees, shrubs and bushes were glowing. Being a rational and pragmatic person I looked for the source of the sunlight, but there was none. So I stopped and gazed in silent amazement and found myself in an amazement of silence which was simply worshipful.

By a piece of irony, serendipity or coincidence, as I walked up the hill into the open country beyond that valley of golden light a cuckoo called. It was the April following the March in which Mrs Thatcher had been condemning my irrelevance as a cuckoo. So I just wandered in wonder and in questioning what I should do next. But I felt strangely elated – and somehow liberated.

As I have continued in my pilgrimage, faith and ministry I have found, especially as I have grown older and more familiar with it, that the seventh strand in my cord is the Bible in its own right and mystery of revelation. As I have gone on seeking to explore Christian faith, apply Christian faith and expound the faith truthfully and effectively for the world we now live in, especially over the last eighteen years or so since I was designated Bishop of Durham, I have realized more than ever just what a reservoir of spiritual struggle and what a source of information and inspiration about the reality and the Spirit of God this biblical collection of heterogeneous texts really is. As to the Old Testament, the texts claim to cover prophetically and faithfully significant matters from the creation of the world through the second millennium BC figures of Abraham and Moses and on into the more historical phase of Israel in Canaan and thus on through the vicissitudes of Israelite and Jewish history. The stories, prophecies and histories, together with the hymns of praise and despair, are inspired comments on, and presentations of, how the people of Israel and the Jews produced many people who encountered God and spoke of him to a people struggling to be the people of God. They are not what we would call history, but stories, myths and reports of prophetic encounters which reflect and resonate with being found by God and therefore having something to share about God.

For Christians the New Testament is a similar but much shorter and very much more condensed commentary on the centrally significant events around the prophetic and disturbing figure of Jesus of Nazareth. All is to be understood in the context of previous faith in God, revelatory encounter now and prospects and possibilities for the future. Thus the Bible is not a depository of once for all data, whether of history or law. Nor does it lay down a necessary interpretation of events and sayings which are always to be taken in one fixed way. In particular the texts are not to be used as always being literally the case, or as making a declaration once and for all that some particular historical tradition has to be true in this way until the end of time. The Bible is an inspired and inspirationally lively library of writings, read and passed on with modifications, amendments and additions, by people who were in the way of faith for the present use and inspiration of the current faithful. It is to be read and reflected on with a view to the corporate knowledge and service of God in the present – always with a view to his everlasting future. Its inspiration and perspectives are to be shared, sought and served by all the faithful with a view to the universalizability for that future in and through the continuing presence and activity of God.

So a regular, attentive and searching use of the Bible, carried on by the faithful both individually and in company deepens, widens and challenges faith. Hence there is a sense in which the regular and devout use of the Bible binds together my sevenfold cord of faith. This cord of faith is also bound together by the shared sacramental worship of the faithful.

Thus my faith, which I recognize as shared with so many across the Bible, across the history and tradition of the church and the churches, and across the world in so many different versions and searchings, is to be received, understood and pursued as a pilgrimage in touch with God into the reality of God and for the promise of his future. Faith is thus received, sustained and lived within an expanding experience of living reality. It is not a taught religion or a series of detached beliefs received on authority.

15 Going on with God

Writing this book has liberated me from being over-concerned with my worry and grief that the church in so many of its forms, and in the behaviour of so many of its faithful, too often puts people off God. My continuing worry and grief has been put in its place by a clear and dynamic vision of the mystery and promise of human beings who have emerged through the processes of the universe with the potential to share in the creativity and love of God.

For the first fifteen to sixteen hundred years of the church's life, no one had any idea of any real possibilities of progress. The world was a place of pilgrimage, where men and women were called to faith in God, to be instructed by the church in ways of life, morals and political obedience which would keep them on the way to eternal life with God. Nothing could be done about the world and the material conditions of life. The practice of religion was about piously *waiting upon God* for eventual salvation and fulfilment. The saeculum or age in which human beings had lived since the incarnation, death and resurrection of Jesus Christ was the last stage before the final end of God's judgement. So the godly way of life was to wait, be faithful and endure until either your own end came in death or God summed everything up in his final end.

My wrestlings with the church, faith and engagement in the

modern world shaped by human science, economics and politics has led me to formulate our need – as Christians and as faithful followers of God – to wake up to the new saeculum.

Since the seventeenth century the human race has experienced a formerly inconceivable explosion of human knowledge. Human beings have developed their capacities to think for themselves and to modify much in the world and in themselves in ways utterly unimaginable until they were discovered and developed *by ourselves.* We have discovered and learned ways of technology, science, trade and productivity which have not only transformed the way we live but have opened up our prospects in previously unthinkable ways.

I urge the Christian churches, who have been the source and sustenance of my Christian faith, to recognize that the time is vastly overdue for all of us Christians to recognize the drastic nature of the achievements of the new saeculum. We, created human beings, live in a modern world surrounded by exciting possibilities (and consequent immense responsibilities) for shaping and modifying the very structures of our lives in body, soul and communities.

I fail to understand why so many people have taken our discoveries, from the vastness of the universe to the micro-biochemical structures of our very bodies, as compelling evidence to *reduce* ourselves to – say – selfish genes or beings whose lives are determined by the necessities of price exchanges in the market. Why this miserable, myopic, self-centred shrinking of vision?

My original concern about the church and the churches stemmed from my conviction that they (we) immeasurably contributed to this secular myopia by a determination to trap the dynamics of God within the self-centred constructions of religion. The enthusiasts of revealed religion have neglected the exciting possibilities of joining creatively in the *new* saeculum which is developing in the West because they insist the modern age is pursuing its way contrary to the way of true faith and is in conflict with God's revelation. Fearing the world, too many of the faithful are diverting their energies into internal quarrels between themselves over details of belief and behaviour. Thus they are drawing the churches and the concerns of faith ever further away from the opportunities of the real world, leaving secular human energy and inspiration to be diverted away from the promising reality of God into dogmatic forms of reductionism. Moral and practical fundamentalisms are not confined to religions; they arise in the name of science and of technology – and still more of economics and politics.

The main message of this book is: 'Oh, come *on* all ye faithful!' We are called to join in God's amazing agenda of unending love with all the grace, guts and intellectual, spiritual, moral energy and insight we can muster. I am convinced that God will multiply our efforts in ever more far-reaching and engaging ways if we will just take the risk. It is odd and sad that religious authorities and strongly religious individuals should expend such energy to protect God and the faithful from risk when the God we worship has taken the colossal risk of creation, following it with incarnation and persevering with engagement, enduring forgiveness and the suffering hope of sacrificial service in and through the Spirit.

In writing this book as part of my pilgrimage of faith I have been revived by the liberation of my faith. It is true that 'Even the church cannot keep a good God down.' This is important for me personally. But of far more importance for us all is a new and refreshing perspective not only on the liberation of faith but on the *scope* of faith. God is indeed committed to all for all. But revelation takes time – it takes time to be recognized and to be received. God has not stopped. He goes steadfastly on. Christians have taken a long time to catch up with where he has moved on to in enabling the development of men and women into the image of God. The creator calls us to be co-creators with him and contributors to the untrammelled energy of God's unending agenda of love. Thus we share in drawing out from the natural processes of an evolving universe the humane and loving purposes of the God who risks his being in order to share love with human beings.

The agenda of God into which we are all called is going on and therefore is in itself unfinished and incomplete. This insight sets us free from any right or need to insist on totally closed and impermeable boundaries between ways of faith and practices of humane service and hope. The faithful need to be faithful enough, patient enough, humble enough to sense the futility and distracting irrelevance of conflicts pursued without compromise. If the mystery of being human flows into the mystery of God, then laying down the law about what is essentially right and who is entirely wrong – most particularly in details – is inappropriate to the ongoing development of humane understanding and action.

This does not, of course, mean that all sorts of practical and far-reaching decisions do not have to be taken as and when required. I have a vivid memory of an encounter during my training as a young artillery officer. A visiting brigadier set me a particular technical problem relating to the use of a troop of four twenty-five pounder guns. In my usual style I began, 'Well, sir, on the one hand this . . . and on the other hand that . . .' 'By god!' he interrupted. 'You'd all be dead by now.' All sorts of decisions have to be taken in good faith when the need arises. But these are tactical questions within the pursuit of some particular plan or purpose. I remain convinced that the ultimate purpose lies in the love and the future of God, so there is always much more for every one of us to discover and share with one another from our particular insights and experiences in the light of the perspective of the future of human being in God.

The process of revelation evolves through pilgrimage and

exploration of our mutual service, shared hopes and practical policies of love and sacrifice, pursued between companies of pilgrims in particular places and cultures. I myself share in the belief that Jesus is the unique and decisive presence of God among us. As such he demonstrates the utter devotion and commitment of God to us. God is for us, God is with us and is one and the same God as the Holy Spirit who is around, between and within us to develop godly hopes and relationships, godly service and perseverance.

I suggest that one way of developing the collaboration between people of differing faith perspectives and differing convictions about the presence or absence of God may very well lie in the adoption of some shared views about the definition and practical interaction between *secularity* and *sacramentality*.

Secularity demands that participants in practical discussions about shared human and social concerns must be careful not to allow particular religious visions, or particular personal perspectives, to intrude into discussion of material processes that are deemed proper matter for scientific investigation and technological manipulation. 'Natural law', for example, is no longer a useful concept because the developments of humane study about the *processes* of 'nature' have enabled men and women to alter and shape 'nature'. Matters of fact are secular matters, not religious ones. But being human, developing humanity and cherishing humaneness are not solely 'matters of fact'. They are 'sacramental', wherever any group or cult or pressure-group expresses values and inspiration about what is 'sacred' – that is, what is of value, of worth, of wonder and of hope.

The collaborative ground between people of differing faiths and perspectives lies in a common definition of, and common respect for, the secular, which will then allow us, all from our various perspectives, to pursue the humane, the wonderful and the worshipful together. Unless we form the habit of practising some humane discipline and respect for differing perspectives on human investigation and investment, we shall simply generate ever more conflict and ever less collaboration. Witness the history of conflict and devastation promoted by faithful adherents of secular ideologies, religious faiths and local nationalisms.

Christians have much to contribute to this wider, deeper and more personal level of human existence because of the understanding and experience of grace, of sacramentality, of forgiveness and of hope that we have developed through our faith in God.

Once the church and the churches grasp the unfinished nature of God's unending agenda of love, then they are free to participate in this ongoing agenda towards the fulfilment of human beings in the love of God without having to insist on closed and definite boundaries between ways of faith and of service to this human future. Christians know God in Jesus through the Holy Spirit to be open to, and concerned with, all. He is therefore equally concerned with Jews or Muslims, Hindus or Buddhists, humanists, atheists and agnostics. Our common concern as human beings is the way forward to a better future in our limited and globalized world.

I believe that the liberating concept is that of *universalizability*. I personally have no doubt that the offer of love which God makes in Jesus through the Spirit is *universal*. But this universal love of God has too often been interpreted as if God had stopped and that nothing fresh of importance could emerge in the relationship between God and human beings. The new saeculum shows that this is not so. Time goes on and so revelation goes on. There is always more to discover, to learn and to put into practice. Universalizability, although an awkward word, means that the universal love of God shown in Jesus has yet to achieve its aim and its full scope. This means that encounters between the faithful and nonbelievers should cease to focus on who converts whom, but on how we contribute from our own ways of faith and understanding to the universal future of the love of all for all things in the love of God.

Christians understand that the glory of human existence is that human beings have the freedom and power to develop in the image of God. God took a risk in creation. Love is always threatened by the misery caused by the misuse of our human powers in selfishness, stupidity and ignorance. Whatever our religious faith, and whatever our own perceptions of the reality of God, we need to come together to address pressing human questions, making our contribution from what resources for human being we have perceived and are seeking to develop.

Our humane mission now – as Christians and as faithful believers in God – is not primarily to convert but to share; not to conflict but to collaborate. We are not called to write off our neighbours but to seek to understand and to contribute some shareable insights into our mission, our hopes and our enjoyments. Where that will get us, God only knows.

The assurance of faith includes the promise that in the end we shall know as we are known. Thus it will prove to be the case that personal human beings – and our like anywhere else in any universe of universes – are not molecular accidents evolved by chance. Our source and resource is not an energy that exploded out of nothing on the way to collapsing into nothing. The mystery is far greater than that. It is we who are discovering all this. Hence the hope, the risk and the wonder of going on.

Appendix 1
The nature of Christian belief [1]

As we argue about what is involved in Christian believing and about whether or not women should be ordained to priesthood in the Christian church, there is one question which is more and more forced upon me and which I therefore feel obliged to share with Synod. The question is this. 'Is our God worth believing in?'

Our God, so it is forcefully argued by some, must have performed certified and guaranteed physical miracles in order that the incarnation can have happened and the resurrection be the real and glorious exposition and explosion of divine power that we all believe it to be. He is a God who must have specially and uniquely intervened to transform very particular particles of matter into a particular divine reality, symbol and mystery. This, it is alleged, was necessary so that God could be one with us in and as the human being Jesus, and in order to deliver Jesus fully and personally and finally from the dead. In the case of the incarnation we are concerned with the divine

1 Speech delivered to the General Synod in York, 6 July 1986, reprinted in *General Synod July Group of Sessions 1986, Report of Proceedings*, Vol. 17, No. 2, pp. 465–71 and in David E. Jenkins, *God, Miracle and the Church of England*, SCM Press 1987.

transformation of Mary's chromosomes and genes so that Jesus is a fully human male and, in and as one and the same person, also Emmanuel, God with us. In the case of the resurrection we have the divine transformation of the particular physical make-up of Jesus' corpse so that he is alive, and seen to be alive, in a transformed body which is the necessary sign and symbol of Jesus' being alive in a manner appropriate to glory and to eternity or in a manner preliminary to, and on the way to, glory and eternity.

The critical point is the claim that the miraculous and divinely produced transformation must be a directly divinely induced transformation of the physical in order for the incarnation and the resurrection to be believable, real and historical. God's power and presence and commitment must, so it is claimed, in these two particular cases have acted something like a divine laser-beam which fuses the physical particles into a reality which is both divinely produced and divine. It is further claimed that the biblical records both support and require this way of understanding incarnation and resurrection and, even today, allow of no other interpretation and exposition as fully appropriate or faithful.

I wish to set aside all the customary critical and comparative questions which arise and which have to be discussed and lived with concerning the New Testament evidences and their interpretation. The question I feel obliged to concentrate on is this. What sort of God are we portraying and believing in if we insist on what I will nickname 'the divine laser-beam' type of miracle as the heart and basis of the incarnation and the resurrection? I feel obliged to suggest that if we do so insist, then we are implying, if not actually portraying, a God who is at the best a cultic idol and at the worst the very devil. Let me try to explain this deeply troubling possibility.

God, it is apparently alleged, works uniquely and directly in a divine intervention on physical matter in order to bring about his basic saving miracles of incarnation and resurrection. Now please be very clear that it is no part of my argument, exploration and meditation to say that it is clear on theoretical or philosophical or scientific grounds that God cannot do that. God is far too great a mystery, and the created universe, in dependence upon him, is far too open a mystery, for it to be possible for any of us to say what God can or cannot do or what can or cannot happen. Still less am I saying that miracles do not or cannot happen. I am wrestling, in the light of God's unique presence in and as Jesus Christ, with what miracles actually are in a realistic and down-to-earth way.

God, in order to declare and achieve our salvation, chose to become one of us. Jesus was the man God chose to become, and this Jesus, as a man, chose to die in obedience to his Father for the sake of God's kingdom and, as we have come to know, for us women and men and for our salvation. This implies and expresses a truly wonderful and utterly gracious identification of God with us. God put himself at our disposal that we might be brought to his disposal. If God is this sort of loving, identifying and gracious God, then surely we must be very careful, reverent and reticent about how we pin certain sorts of miracle on him.

The choice of physical miracles with what might be called laser-beam-like precision and power would not seem to be a choice which he cared, or would care, to use. For if such a physical transformation with precision and power is an option open to God consistent with his purposes of creation, freedom and love, then we are faced with a very terrible dilemma indeed. We are faced with the claim that God is prepared to work knock-down physical miracles in order to let a select number of people into the secret of his incarnation, resurrection and salvation, but he is not prepared to use such methods in order to deliver from Auschwitz, prevent Hiroshima, overcome famine or bring about a bloodless transformation of apartheid. Such a God is surely a cultic idol. That is to say, he is a false and misdeveloped picture of the true and gracious God drawn up by would-be worshippers who have gone dangerously and sadly astray. If such a God is not a cultic idol produced by mistaken and confused worshippers, but actually exists, then he must be the very devil. For he prefers a few selected worshippers to all the sufferers of our world. Such a God is certainly not worth believing in. But I do not believe that we can possibly so have learned Christ.

In fact and in faith, God's relations with the world and with ourselves, including his miracles, are surely something much more mysterious, personal and risky than the knock-down, this-must-be-a-decisive-physical miracle, type of argument and understanding allow. Miracles are most probably something much more historical, real and down-to-earth than monophysitely divine manipulations of the physical. God is much more interwoven with and committed to our flesh and blood, our obedience and collaboration and our freedom and limits. He transforms the natural, not by making it arbitrarily supernatural and so unnatural, but by enabling the unbelievable fullness of what is natural through unity with the unbelievably gracious divine. The birth narratives are far more about the obedience of Mary and Joseph in response to the unique graciousness of God than about Mary's physical virginity. The resurrection narratives are far more about encounters and namings and joyful recognitions than about the empty tomb. Miracles are gifts rather than guarantees, given to faith and perceived by faith, and they always involve a mysterious collaboration and convergence between the intervening power of God and human responses of faith, obedience and activity.

We are always wanting to pin God down by getting things cut and dried and decisive. God is always wanting to set us free to share in the mystery and the suffering of creation, freedom and redemption. God undertook the cross when he undertook creation. We – and especially religious people organized into churches – are always trying to limit the risk, curtail the openness, contract the freedom and avoid that commitment of faith which is the falling into the risk and abyss of love. I realize that it is stupid and foolish of me to attempt mystical theology in a debate in Synod. But surely we cannot avoid such a folly, for we are debating (must we be debating – could we not be exploring?) faith and the role of women in the church before the mystery of God as this has been declared to us in the face of Jesus Christ.

So to be true and faithful to tradition we must think about the central mysteries of our faith in a way which takes full account of where we now are in our contemporary world. For the central mystery of the incarnation is that God took on the contemporary world. He is not a once-visiting God who froze somewhere between the first and fourth centuries. Tradition is not a noun shaped once and for all in the past; it is a verb active under God now for the sake of the future.

And in so taking on the world, God made it clear that he is not a triumphalistic God who produces knock-down miraculous arguments. He is a being-with and suffering-through God who again and again produces miracles of collaboration and transcendence, all in the midst of our suffering, struggling and oddly glorious world. So the final point of my meditation in mystical theology is this. As he is not a triumphalistic God, he does not have a triumphalistic church.

It simply is not true that there is anywhere a church which is guaranteed to get it right under God. As there are no knock-down miracles which prove to everybody that God is around, so there is no church with knock-down authority which can settle decisively and definitely for ever what God is like and what God wants. To claim this, or to behave as if this were so, is to present an impossible and unworthy picture of God. For if it were the case that there exists a church which is bound to be right when it speaks for God, speaks of God or acts for God, then we should all be bound to be atheists. For the records of all churches contain acts of inhumanity, declarations of stupidity and indications of triumphalism, arrogance and insensitivity which are a disgrace to God – or, indeed to ordinary humanity. It is surely quite clear that it is practically and morally impossible to believe in an ecclesiastical God or a God of the church. God must be far more than, and at times very distanced from, the church or all churches. We worship God, not the church in any shape or form. That was one of the most fundamental reassertions of Protestantism and of the Reformation, and it has to be reasserted again and again. This sort of Protestantism is an essential part of catholic and apostolic faith and practice. Within, under and through this worship of God we thankfully accept that there is a church of God, which he calls, judges, changes and sustains and – above all – mercifully and graciously uses. There is a church of God but there is no God of the church. He is the God of the whole earth and mystery of all things. We belong to him, but he does not belong to us. He identifies himself with us and saves us, but he is sovereign, free, glorious and mysterious.

Two practical postcripts follow, to which I can refer only in a sentence or two, but which deserve our most careful investigation. The first is that it is essential, at any rate for the time being, to preserve the distinctive nature and identity of Anglicanism. We are not papalist Roman and we are not biblicist Protestant. We are clear that all churches err, have erred and will err. We are also clear, however, about the importance of traditional creeds, traditional ministry and being kept together by our worship and our ministry. We rely on God to keep us together, correct us together and move us forward together. For Christian life and witness in the church, belonging is more important than agreeing and it is more important to live, worship and work together than to be in the right. As we live together we shall work out, under God, developing understanding of what is required by our worship of God, Father, Son and Holy Spirit, and of how we embody and express mutually recognized patterns of faith and of baptism, eucharist and received ministry. It is urgently necessary, however, that we remain clear that belonging together is more important than agreeing. God gives himself to us through one another and our differences as much as through Bible or tradition, or a particular way of ordering and practising things. It is the living body which counts. And we need to be clear that living together and serving the world is more important than being right or in the right.

Which leads to the second practical point. We are saved by grace through faith and we have no righteousness of our own. Therefore we are not prevented from being part of the true church, and being fully received by our fellows, by the errors which we make, just as the Church of Rome is not prevented from being part of the true church of God by having made the nearly disastrous error of claiming in 1870 to have an infallible authority. Sin does not have dominion over us. So we are always free to live together, work things out together and to change. We do not have to wait for papal authority to do this. Our concern is not with the past of the Roman church but with the future of the whole church of God. We look, therefore, for the eventual close unity when all have repented and changed.

Therefore we know that whatever our responsibly considered decisions and whatever our worked-out expressions of faith and of order, we are saved by God as much despite them as because of them. We are not able – until the End – to serve God in *his* way. We can serve God only in our respective and imperfect ways which he accepts, blesses, judges, forgives and changes. We need one another, and none of us is in the right.

So we ought to accept the report from the House of Bishops and move on in conversation, commitment, criticism and witness. We need to face the issue of the ordination of women and not be bullied, frightened or dismayed by backward-looking references to tradition or being bound by a past in which God no longer lives. He lives now and for the future. Above all we need to pray very earnestly that God will, of his very great mercy, spare us the ultimate humiliation and horror of discussing him and deciding about the ordering of a part of his church in ways which deny his mystery, his freedom, his infinite openness and his incredibly suffering love.

Appendix 2
The ordination of women[1]

I wonder if we have reached the point in this Synod, as we come near to the vote, where we have to stop being balanced in our attempts to understand and argue with one another. Ought we not perhaps rather to be broken by the shame we are bringing on God, his Christ and the gospel? Is it not shameful to be quarrelling as we are about women in the church when the whole world is torn by poverty, strife and lostness, and to be doing it in the full glare of the media?

Is it not disgraceful that we have so little faith in the catholicity of Christ's incarnation for all and in the catholicity of the sacrament of his body and blood that we confine that sacrament to men's hands? Surely women's hands are as human and as able to be hallowed by God's grace and calling?

Should we not perhaps feel ashamed and angry that we talk blandly about pain on both sides and we are advised not to be angry about whatever comes from this vote? For a No vote condemns us

1 Speech delived to the General Synod, 11 November 1992, reprinted in *General Synod November Group of Sessions 1992, Report of Proceedings*, Vol. 23, No. 3, pp. 763–5.

to five more years of wasted energy, and consigns called, tested and trusted women in our diaconate and elsewhere to more years of condescension and, I do honestly fear, oppression. How can we not be angry?

Yet I know – and I mean that I *know* – in the fabric of my being that the persons in my diocese who oppose this legislation include priests who are devoted and disciplined priests with whom I personally share a zeal for the gospel and for Christ's sacraments. They will be angry if this legislation is passed.

How are we to respond to all this? It brings me near to despair when our church so obscures the glories of the gospel at such a time of need and opportunity. It nearly breaks my heart, for I have been long enough in my diocese to care that my women deacons should be freed for their priestly calling and not be left in distress, and also to care that my opposing brethren should not be separated and put into distress.

Do we not have to realize that to be near to despair and to be threatened with a broken heart is to be very near where Christ has been before, and so to understand that there can still be saving grace if we seek to live together by forgiveness? We have to choose: to follow the majority in becoming free to ordain women to the priesthood, or to be blocked for the time being by the minority. Can we not throw ourselves on the mercy of God by choosing to go ahead in humility, confusion, distress and togetherness? Not of course beyond all reasonable doubt, for who is ever there, but together in reasonable hope and faith. With the complexities of our two-thirds voting system in three different Houses, the result of our vote will in any case be something like a statistical chance. We shall achieve not the will of God but the opportunity to find out where he wills to take us, whatever the outcome.

Is it not Anglican to leave theological loose ends and questions yet to be answered? The accompanying legislation that we have is, I am sure, flawed, but it has been offered for honourable and Anglican reasons. We know that we must choose to ordain or not to ordain, but we refuse to choose to exclude disagreeing brothers and sisters. We are not trying to square an impossible circle but to live openly to one another by the possibilities of God's enabling grace.

I hope, therefore, that we will muster the necessary majorities to go ahead with this legislation, but surely we may all be free to vote faithfully in all humility as we judge we must. This is because we know that, whatever the result of the vote, we have not yet got the will of God. We shall only have the opportunity together to go on seeking his will, receiving his grace and offering him service.

Surely, brothers and sisters in Christ, it cannot be that our vote will destroy the being, worship and service of the church. It cannot be so, simply because of forgiveness: God will enable and renew. It cannot be so, because of simple catholicity: God will continue his universal purposes and honour his universal sacraments. It cannot be so, simply because God has called us: we must vote as we must, and then we must continue together, in humility, in hope and in the forgiving and empowering grace of God.

Index

189

Index

Index